MW00586491

"I live in hope that the world u
equality for everyone, regardless
Redhead Encyclopedia may help
(Eric Stoltz - actor, "Pulp Fictio.., ..ou ..oy, The Prophecy")

"I'm enclosing a recent issue of MAD magazine to show you that our
mascot, Alfred E. Neuman, is a redhead...
(William Gaines, Publisher MAD Magazine)

"We would like to thank Stephen Douglas' Redhead Encyclopedia for
providing Jeopardy clues concerning "Famous Redheads." We always
try to refer to sources as close to the original as possible...
(George Vosburgh, producer JEOPARDY!)

"The Redhead Encyclopedia makes for terrific reading ... so many
facts I was not aware of."
(Scott Grimes - actor, star of Fox's "Party of Five" TV series and
motion picture "Critters.")

"I've served alongside Aussie troops and they called the redheads
'Blueys!' Enjoyed your book!"
(Brian Keith - actor, "Family Affair," "Magruder & Loud")

"What Clairol did for blondes, Stephen Douglas and Redheads
International has done for redheads."
(Tova Borgnine, owner of Tova Cosmetics and Ernie's wife)

"...The Redhead Encyclopedia truly is an outstanding piece of work.
Clearly, you are the world leader in the promotion of our select
fellowship!"
(Duane Abbajay - CEO / JFR International Cosmetics)

"When Contributing Photographer Richard Fegley set about shooting
this month's pictorial "Reds," he got an insider's view of one
spectacular minority group from Stephen Douglas, president of
Redheads International Club."
(PLAYBILL - Playboy Magazine)

"I believe that if there is no road, make one. The Redhead
Encyclopedia is eerie, but wonderful!"
(Michael Kopelow - actor, "The Stoned Age," "Point Break,"
"Don't Tell Mom The Babysitter's Dead")

"I enjoyed reading your book!"
(Jacklyn Zeman, actress - Bobby Spencer on "General Hospital")

THE REDHEAD ENCYCLOPEDIA

Compiled and Written by

Stephen Douglas

Published by
*Redheads International in association with the
StoneCastle Literary Group*

COVER DESIGN: JOHN MEL/PRINTWORKS

Sheet music covers provided by Sandy Marrone
Sheet Music Specialist
113 Oakwood Drive
Cinnaminson, NJ 08077

ISBN# 0-9645216-0-1 THE REDHEAD ENCYCLOPEDIA

Redheads International • 537 Newport Center Drive #119, Newport Beach,
CA 92660. Direct orders of this book may be made at this address by sending
$19.95 plus $3.00 for postage and handling to Redheads International.

PRINTED IN THE UNITED STATES OF AMERICA

PREFACE

"As one redhead to another, what in the world are you trying to sell me?" (Arthur Godfrey to Lucille Ball - "The Lucy Show")

As the president and founder of Redheads International, a national organization for redhead promotion and celebration, I started out with the intention of compiling redhead facts and interesting stories that had landed in my office from all over the world. I needed to save time - I had been writing long-winded letters back to people, including other writers wishing to write redhead books, reporters and students needing material for their reports, and the Kinsey Institute, who wanted "all the information on redheads" that I had. From the desire to consolidate my information and make the process easier, this book was born.

As I began filtering through this information, I started to see a myriad of coincidences between red-follicled humans and greatness. Settling in at the library, I was sorely unamused that looking in the reference books, "redhead" didn't get me any more information that I already knew: *"Redhead - person having redhair."* This hardly provided details on the rich diversities inherent in the experiences and history of redheads. (I admit that the Oxford Dictionary, the "SuperBowl" of dictionaries, provided much more detail on the word "red".)

So as I cross-referenced some of the earlier facts I had gathered with the new resources, such as the library's book and magazine periodical listings, I began to uncover some great material. Suddenly, I was engulfed in a flurry of information popping up here and there, one thing leading to another. Students at the library were slowly rearranging themselves away from me, shaking their heads in pity at my muffled outbursts of surprise and exclamations each time I found another interesting redhead tidbit.

It has been a very enlightening experience for me, one that was wholly unexpected. I hope that everyone who chances to view these redhaired revelations will be uncontrollably forced to notice redheads, gaze at them and say "wow, there's another redhead," and give honor to their forgotten place in history. I want to thank the good librarians at the Santa Ana, Newport Beach, El Toro and Irvine Libraries (California) for their considerations and help in giving me needed assistance in finding the information for the completion of this book.

In Memorium

Sheldon Ream
Greg Bland
John Scarantino
Barry Weir

Dedication

This book is dedicated to everyone who has been good to me and the redhead celebration - so with no real intention of brevity; My mom and dad, Albert, Ann Lauren, Darryl & Sandy and the boys, Geoff Perlman, Pete, Jim, my sister and a redhaired cast of thousands.

CROWNED
Dedicated to redhaired Amy George (in memorium 1968-1984)

RED is one of the primary colors
RED is said to signify fortitude and magnanimity
RED is the color of magic throughout the world

The caps of fairies and the jackets of gnomes are RED.
RED is regarded as the color of radicalism
RED is the color of Royalty

Brotherhood is painted on shields of RED
RED describes the purest of gold
RED is the color of danger
RED is the color of revolution
RED is the color of blood, elixir of Life

Excitement is swathed in RED
RED is the color of passion
RED is the color of the heart
RED is warmth and fire, and of the Sun
RED is the announcement of presence
To be RED haired is to wear the Crown of Life, Energy, and Love.

Stephen Douglas

TABLE OF CONTENTS

Chapter One

Chapter Two

Chapter Three

Chapter Four

Chapter Five

Chapter Six

WHAT IS RED?

red (red) n.
1.a. Color. The hue of the long-wave end of the visible spectrum, evoked in the human observer by radiant energy with wavelengths of approximately 630 to 750 nanometers; any of a group of colors that may vary in lightness and saturation and whose hue resembles that of blood; one of the additive or light primaries; one of the psychological primary hues. b. A pigment or dye having a red hue. c. Something that has a red hue.

—red adj. red-der, red-dest.
1. Color. Having a color resembling that of blood.
2. Reddish in color or having parts that are reddish in color: a red dog; a red oak.
3. Having a reddish or coppery skin color.
4. Having a ruddy or flushed complexion: red with embarrassment.

–reudh-. Important derivatives are: red, rufous, robust, corroborate, rambunctious, ruddy, rust, rouge, rubeola, ruby, rubric, russet.
reudh. Red, ruddy.*roudh.*

1.a. RED, from Old English. RORQUAL, from Old Norse *raudhr*, red. From Germanic *raudaz*.

2. ROWAN, from a source akin to Old Norse *reynir*, mountain ash, *rowan* (from its red berries), from Germanic *raudnia*.

1

3. RUFESCENT, RUFOUS, from Latin *rufus* (of dialectal Italic origin), reddish.

4. RUBIGINOUS, from Latin *råbus*, red.

5. ROBLE, ROBORANT, ROBUST; CORROBORATE, (RAMBUNCTIOUS), from Latin *råbur*, *råbus*, red oak, hardness, and *råbustus*, strong.

1. a. RUDDLE, from Old English *rudu*, red color; b. RUDDOCK, from Old English *rudduc*, robin; c. RUDDY, from Old English *rudig*, ruddy. a, b, and c all from Germanic *rudå*.

2. Suffixed form *rudh-sto-. RUST, from Old English *rust*, rust, from Germanic *rust-.

3. ROUGE, RUBEOLA, RUBY; RUBEFACIENT, from Latin *rubeus*, red.

4. RUBICUND, from Latin *rubicundus*, red, ruddy.

5. RUBIDIUM, from Latin *rubidus*, red.

6. Suffixed (stative) form *rudh- RUBESCENT, from Latin *rubtre*, to be red.

7. Suffixed form *rudh-ro-. a. RUBELLA, RUBRIC; BILIRUBIN, from Latin *ruber*, red; b. RUTILANT, from Latin *rutilus*, reddish; c. ERYTHEMA, ERYTHRO-, from Greek *eruthros*, red (with prothetic vowel, from oldest root form *õreudh-); d. ERYSIPELAS, from possibly re-made Greek *erusi-*, red, reddening.

2

8. Suffixed form *rudh-to-. RISSOLE, ROUX, RUSSET, from Latin *russus*, red. [Pokorny reudh- 872.]
(Source - American Heritage Dictionary)

red-head (red'hed') n. a person with red hair.

redhaired - otherwise called "hirsutorfous," "rufous," [latin], or "xanthous," having "pyrrhotism."
(Source - Sisson's Word & Expression Locater)

"The precise shades of color to which red is applied range from bright scarlet or crimson to reddish yellow (golden)..."
(Source - Oxford Dictionary of English Proverbs)

Ways to Describe "Red"

apple cheeks	coral
auburn	coriander
blood	cramoisy
bloom	crimson
blowzy	dawn
blush	erubescent
burgundy	ferruginous
candy-apple-red	fevered
cardinal-red	fiery
carmine	fire
carnation	fire-engine red
carnelian	fireglow
carrot-top	flame
cerise	flame-colored
cherry	flesh-colored
cherry-red	flesh-pink
claret	florid

3

flush
fuchsia
fuchsine
garnet
glow
gore
high color
hot
hot pink
magenta
maroon
Mars
oxblood
painted
peach-colored
pink
poppy
port
purple
red
red-cheeked
red-haired
red-hot
red as a beet
red as a lobster
redbreast
reddish
redhead
Red Indian
red ink
redman
Red Planet
redskin

redbreast
rose
rose-pink
roseate
rosy
rosy-fingered dawn
rosy cheeks
rouged
rubefaction
rubescence
rubicund
rubicundity
rubiginous
rubric
ruby
ruddy
rufescent
rufous
russet
rust-colored
rusty
sandy
sanguine
scarlet
shocking-pink
strawberry
sunset
titian
tomato
Tyrian purple
vermilion
warm
wine-colored

Paint the Town Red

Locations in the United States and Canada named "Red" or "Auburn".

ALABAMA - Auburn, Red Bay, Red Level
ARIZONA - Red Rock
CALIFORNIA - Auburn, Red Bluff, Red Hill, Redlands, Redway, Redwood City
COLORADO - Redcliff, Red Feather
FLORIDA - Auburndale
ILLINOIS - Auburn, Red Bud
INDIANA - Auburn, Redkey
IOWA - Redfield, Red Oak
KENTUCKY - Auburn
LOUISIANA - Red Oaks, Red River, Baton Rouge
MAINE - Auburn
MASSACHUSETTS - Auburn
MICHIGAN - Auburn, Auburn Hills, Redford Township
MINNESOTA - Red Lake, Red Wing, Redwood, Redwood Falls
MISSISSIPPI - Red Banks
MONTANA - Red Lodge
NEBRASKA - Auburn, Red Cloud, Red Willow
NEW JERSEY - Red Bank
NEW MEXICO - Red River
NEW YORK - Auburn, Red Hook, Red Oaks
NORTH CAROLINA - Red Springs
OHIO - Redbird
OKLAHOMA - Red Oak
PENNSYLVANIA - Auburn, Red Hill, Red Lion
TENNESSEE - Red Bank, Red Boiling Springs
TEXAS - Red Oak, Red River, Redwater
UTAH - Redwood
WASHINGTON - Auburn
WEST VIRGINIA - Red Jacket
WISCONSIN - Redgranite
(CANADA) ALBERTA - Red Cliff, Red Deer, Redwater
ONTARIO - Red Rock

REDHEAD PHENOMENA

No other word describing a color is so descriptive, so powerful, and so commonly used, than the word "red". It depicts the most potent color, an adjective that carries strong meanings to many words and phrases ("red dog," "red letter," "red alert," etc.), and can never be connected with anything dull or humdrum.

Being a redhead can be used to one's advantage, as history shows that many past and current redhaired individuals excelled in accomplishing their goals. Can any redhead harness the energy of their hair and use it for constructive and beneficial purposes? Maybe, but one thing is certain, you are fortunate to be born with redhair.

Sometimes maligned, sometimes adored, redheads have had to learn to account for themselves as standouts and beacons of individuality. Realizing the combined creative and social contributions that redheads have given to the world is enough to make any redhead see a potential for greatness germinating within them. If you have a vivid imagination and a propensity to see things differently than the way they might normally look, it would be easy to imagine an ancient race of predominately redhaired people who were technologically and culturally advanced.

However, it is not this book's purpose to prove any theory about a singular class of people who had redhair, but to provide a comprehensive source of information on redheads. Some people may deduce from this book that redheads indeed are a special breed. As far as redheads being a distinct (and now near extinct) race of people, it's not that farfetched. Take the true story of Easter Island, for instance . . .

○ ○

Over 350 years ago, Dutch Admiral Jacob Roggeveen landed on Easter Island, a seemingly barren rock 2,300 miles off the coast of Chile. Known locally as "Rapa Nui," Roggeveen named the island in honor of Easter, the day on which he discovered it. Roggeveen was enroute to find the rumored land of Australia when he decided to stop at the uncharted isle for water and supplies.

As his ships approached the island, Roggeveen and his crew were awestruck at the vision that awaited them – hundreds of huge stone heads, some as large as thirty-five feet tall and weighing as much as 50 tons, stared down at them!

The seafarers were even more surprised when they met the natives of the island. The natives, of Polynesian descent, were described as being "tall, well-built and of good proportions. Only some have black hair; that of the others have a reddish or cinnamon tinge."

The natives of Easter Island had the only ideologic script for writing in Polynesia. They carved this script into stone tablets and into some of the stone heads. The looming stone figures, called *moai*, are made of volcanic ash, but archaeologists are unsure on how the natives moved the huge stone heads into position.

What is even more mysterious is the fact that the Rapa Nui carved huge crowns out of red lava and hoisted them on top of the stone heads.

The moai were used in religious ceremonies

given in honor of Maki Maki, the Sun God. The Rapa Nui men competed in a contest to become the high priest by being the first to find a rare bird egg on the island. The first native to find the egg painted his head red and was given access to supernatural powers, called *mana*, a power from the sun. Mana was thought by many of the natives to have been the force that was used to place the hundreds of heavy stone heads around the island. The natives did not offer Roggeveen any other theory or story for this feat of their forefathers except that the chosen priest, who had his power for a year, was the one who moved the great stone heads with only his words.

It is interesting to note that the mystical connection between redheads and the sun was again reinforced by the Rapa Nui, as in many other cultures in early history, including the Egyptians.

The "cinnamon-haired" natives of Easter Island eventually disappeared as they were traded away as slaves by the white explorers or died of diseases introduced by traders. Today there are approximately 2,500 inhabitants remaining on the island, most of them of Polynesian descent.

° °

There is some conjecture, folklore, and even outright fables about redheads and their unusual but special relationship to the course of human events. This book will attempt to deal with much of it, and provide enough factual information for you to form your own opinions. There are more truths in this book than speculation, and many of those truths deal with the influence that redhaired people had on

8

civilization. I found some interesting statistics: even though only 2% of the population in the world consists of redheads, almost 30% of all the famous and influential people in western history were redheads or came from redheaded families!

Some of these names of redhaired people listed below are mentioned in further detail later in the book. There is no particular order to their listing other than alphabetical:

FAMOUS REDHEADS LIST

Alexander the Great - *mighty ruler of Mesopotamia*
Alexandra of Russia - *Empress*
Algernon Charles Swinburne - *rugged poet*
Andrew Jackson - *President of the United States*
Anton Chekhov - *writer*
Antonio Vivaldi - *composer*
Augustin Daly - *American playwright*
Balboa - *explorer*
Barbarossa - *Moorish pirate*
Bernadette Devlin - *radical*
Beverly Sills - *opera singer*
Billy Wilder - *writer*
Billy the Kid - *1870's American gunslinger*
Calvin Coolidge - *US President*
Cesare Borgia - *military leader*
Charlemagne - *Holy Roman Emperor*
Charles Bickford - *actor*
Charles XII of Sweden - *King*
Charles de Gaulle - *President of France*
Charles VIII of France - *King*
Charlotte Corday - *French Revolutionary heroine*
Christopher Columbus - *explorer*
Cleopatra - *Queen of Egypt*
Clovis - *military leader*
Colonel James Travis - *leader of the Alamo*
Cyrano de Bergerac - *poet swordsman*
D H Lawrence - *writer*
Danny Kaye - *actor and comedian*

Darius the Great - *King of Persia*
Desifi Bernadette - *Queen of Sweden*
Drew Pearson - *football player*
Ed Crump - *Strong boss*
Edna St. Vincent Millay - *American Poet and Pulitzer Prize winner*
Edward IV - *King of England*
Edward II - *King of England*
Eleanor Roosevelt - *First Lady, wife of FDR*
Elinor Glyn - *British writer*
Emily Dickinson - *poet*
Emperor Franz Josef - *King of Austria*
Eric the Red - *Nordic explorer*
Ezra Pound - *author*
F. Scott Fitzgerald - *author*
Francis I of Austria - *King*
Frank Lloyd Wright - *world-renowned architect*
Frederick I - *King of Germany and Emperor*
Frederick II - *King of Germany and Emperor*
Galileo - *scientist*
Garibaldi - *military leader*
General William Clark *(of Lewis and Clark expedition)*
George Washington - *First President of the United States*
George Bernard Shaw - *Irish-born British playwright and Nobel Prize winner*
George Armstrong Custer - *General/U.S. Calvary*
Georgiana - *Duchess of Devonshire*
Glenda Jackson - *actress*
Greer Garson - *actress*
Gwen Verdon - *actress*
Henri IV of France - *King*
Henri Matisse - *painter*
Henry II - *King of England*
Henry VIII - *King of England*
Henry the Navigator - *Explorer*
Huey Long - *labor leader*
Hugh O'Donnell - *last of the Irish Kings*
Ignace Paderewski - *composer*
Isabella of Spain - *Queen*
James Cagney - *actor*
James Russell Lowell - *poet*
Jean Paul Sartre - *philosopher*
Jeremiah Johnson - *pioneer*

Jesus - *Holy man, Son of God*
Jim Bowie - *defender at the Alamo*
John of Gaunt - *Ruler of England*
John D. Rockefeller - *philanthropist*
Joseph Kennedy *(father of John, Edward, and Robert Kennedy)*
Joseph E. Smith - *Mormon founder*
Judas Iscariot - *Traitor disciple of Jesus Christ*
Juliana - *Queen of Netherlands*
Katharine Hepburn- *actress*
King Pyrrhus - *King of Epirus*
Kublai Khan - *military leader*
Lady Nancy Astor - *British politician*
Lady Sarah Churchill - *wife of Winston Churchill*
Leonardo Di Vinci - *famous inventor and painter*
Leif Ericson - *Explorer and son of Eric the Red*
Lily Langtry - *actress of the 1800's*
Lizzie Borden - *alleged ax murderess*
Lord Byron - *poet*
Lorenzo De Medici - *military leader*
Louis XIV of France - *King*
Ludwig I of Bavaria - *King*
Lynn Redgrave - *actress*
Maccha - *Queen of Ireland*
Maggie Smith - *actress*
Malcolm X - *black leader*
Margaret Tudor - *Queen of Scotland*
Marie Antoinette - *French royalty*
Mark Twain - *America's most beloved writer and author*
Marquis de Lafayette - *French military officer*
Marquis de Sade - *writer*
Marquis of Queensbury - *British boxing promoter*
Martin Van Buren - *President of the United States*
Mary of Tudor - *Queen of England*
Mary Smart - *Queen of Scots*
Maureen O'Hara - *actress*
Maureen O'Sullivan - *actress*
Miles Standish - *leader of the early U.S colonies*
Mrs. Karl Marx - *wife of famous philosopher*
Myrna Loy - *actress*
Napoleon Bonaparte - *military leader*
Nell Gwynn - *actress & mistress to a king*
Nero - *Emperor of Rome*

Oliver Cromwell - *statesman*
Otto von Bismarck - *statesman*
Peter the Great - *Tsar of Russia*
Pharaoh Ramses - *King of Egypt*
Ponce de Leon - *explorer*
Queen Elizabeth I - *Queen of England*
Red Laver - *Australian tennis champ*
Red Buttons - *comedian*
Red Grange - *football hero*
Red Skelton - *comedian*
Redd Foxx - *comedian*
Rhonda Fleming - *actress*
Richard I - *King of England*
Richard II - *King of England*
Richard de Burgh - *"The Redde Earl of Ulster"*
Robert Bruce - *King of Scotland*
Robert Edwin Peary - *American Explorer*
Rominov of Russia - *Empress*
Ron Howard - *actor, director*
Roxana - *wife of Alexander the Great*
Rufus Matthew Jones - *American Quaker philosopher*
Rupert Brooke - *poet*
Rurik of Novgorod - *Grand Duke of Kiev*
Salome - *Biblical seductress*
Sarah Bernhardt - *famous actress*
Sinclair Lewis - *writer*
Sir Walter Raleigh - *explorer*
Sir Osbert Sitwell - *British writer*
Spencer Tracy - *actor*
St. Bernard of Clairvouix - *French monastic reformer*
Susan Clark - *actress*
Svetlana Stalin - *Russian writer/daughter of Josef* Stalin
Tallulah Bankhead - *actress*
Taylor Caldwell - *novelist*
Thomas Jefferson - *3rd President and statesman*
Thomas Hardy - *writer*
Thor - *mythic god*
Titian - *painter of redheads*
Tycho Brahe - *Danish astronomer*
Vanessa Redgrave - *actress*
Vincent Van Gogh - *painter*
Vivien Leigh - *actress*

Vladimir Lenin - *revolutionary leader of Russia*
Wallenstein - *military leader*
Walter Reuther - *founder of labor unions*
Wilhelmina - *Queen of Netherlands*
William Blake - *writer*
William Rufus II - *King of England*
William Shakespeare - *premier writer*
William the Conqueror - *King of England*
William the Silent - *King of Germany*
Winston Churchill - *British leader*
Woody Allen - *actor, producer, writer/director*
Xerxes - *King of the Persian Empire*

REDHEAD COLOR SCALE

There are many shades of redhair. This book recognizes the following descriptions of red shades to be considered as "redhair":

Straw Red	- light reddish blonde
Golden Red	- light bright red
Orange Red	- bright red
Copper	- metallic, shiny red
Titian	- deep red
Auburn	- dark red
Russet	- brownish red
Chestnut	- red brunette

John Paul Jones

Chapter One

HISTORICAL FIGURES

Many of the most prominent figures throughout history were redheads. The House of Tudor, for example, brought forth an abundance of crimson-crowned Kings, Queens, Princes, Princesses, Earls, Dukes, and other redheads with titles of nobility.

During the Middle Ages, being a redhead made you suspect of having magical powers, and you might travel a road to respect or derision depending on the position you held in life. Redhair could be a detriment or a benefit because the extreme color of your hair garnered attention in a mystical sense during those times. The individual ability to harness that attention was what made these redheads great.

EXPLORERS

Eric the Red - (late 10th Century AD) A Norwegian adventurer who discovered Greenland, Eric was born and raised in Jaeren, Norway, but was expelled from there after committing murder. He was still respected as a Viking warrior and was given much leeway within the law, but he decided to leave Norway at his enemies' urging and was forced to settle in Iceland. Somewhat of a hothead, he murdered a few more men and was forced to leave Iceland, too. He discovered a new country during his flight from Iceland and later started a Viking settlement there. To make it sound enticing to prospective colonists, Eric the Red named his new land, "Greenland," even though it was mainly covered with glaciers and rock.

His wife and family converted to Christianity, but Eric remained attached to his wild pagan ways. His son, redhaired **Leif Ericson**, was more respectable, and wanted Eric to accompany him on an exploration of new lands.

On the way to his ship, Eric fell off his horse and injured his foot. Taking it for a bad omen, he refused to go on the trip with his son. Subsequently, Leif left with out him and discovered North America, saved the lives of a shipwrecked Viking party on his way back home, was given their booty, and took over rulership of Greenland. When Eric died during an epidemic, Leif was a respected and rich man, a result of his sailing heroics, subsequently giving him the nickname "Leif the Lucky".

Christopher Columbus - Christopher Columbus was using an alias and he also didn't discover America, comes the startling news from the book "The New Columbus" by author Frederick J. Pohl. Actually born Juan Colon on the Spanish island of Majorca, Christopher Columbus was described as "a princely type," tall and Nordic, with blue eyes and redhair.

When he was a young man, he raided Spanish ships as a privateer for Portugal, until he got the idea of sailing to the East with the dream of building himself a wealthy empire. He needed funds to make the trip and was first turned down by the Portuguese because they wanted to make the trip themselves.

In order to approach the Spanish with his plan, he

had to take a different identity, one similar to his friend Christoforo Colombo. His requests for funds was eventually granted and he was finally commissioned by Spanish Queen Isabel to take the trip.

When Juan (Columbus) successfully returned from his adventure to the Americas, he had to adopt a Genoan name to continue his masquerade as an Italian. His letters to his friends even had to be translated into Italian.

He was a dashing fellow and probably the best navigator of his day, even though he didn't "discover" America. (There's even a dispute as to which island he really landed on first). Columbus led an adventurous life, making at least three trips from Spain to the New World he was thought to have discovered.

Fernando Cortez - (1485-1547) A Spanish conquistador, Cortez is one of the major discoverers of the Americas. He captured Mexico when he was sent on a commission from Cuban governor Diego de Velazquez to conquer Montezuma and the Aztecs.

When Cortez reached the Aztec capital of Tenochtitlán, Montezuma received him after thinking he was a descendent from the god Quetzalcoatl. Cortez took Montezuma hostage and ruled the Aztecs for a short while. His forces suffered heavy losses when the Aztecs revolted, but Cortez regrouped and attacked several months later, destroying the Aztec capital and much of their civilization. He returned to Spain and asked Charles V to make him governor of Mexico. The king refused, and Cortez died before returning to his conquered land.

ALEXANDER THE GREAT

MILITARY LEADERS

Alexander the Great - (356-323 B.C) The legendary king of Macedonia, Alexander "had the hair of a lion with one blue eye and one black." He was the greatest conqueror of the ancient world over two thousand years ago. He captured Persia from Darius III, and went on to found Alexandria in Egypt, control Greece, and northern India. By the 17th Century, over eighty versions of his story existed in 24 different languages. His wife Roxana was also rumored to be a redhead.

Napoleon I - (1769-1821) As the Emperor of France, he was a fierce military man, but too impulsive to be a truly wise leader. He was very insecure about his small height and because of his legendary stubbornness, today the term "napoleonic complex" has come to sometimes be used to unfairly stereotype short people who are strong-willed. His last battle was also the reason behind the apocryphal phrase, "met his Waterloo," referring to his debilitating defeat at Waterloo in Russia.

After his debacle in Russia, he quickly left his French Army in the field to hurry home, fearing his popularity might be in jeopardy with his people. At the bank of a river, he asked the ferryman, "Have there been many French deserters?" The ferryman replied, "No, you are the first."

Rufus Putnam - (1738-1824) American Revolutionary soldier who became a hero when he directed the placement of artillery on Dorchester Heights and forced the British armies to evacuate Boston in 1775.

John Paul Jones - (1747-92) Called the "Father of the U.S. Navy," John Paul Jones was a high-strung man who never gave up. After joining a sailing ship at fourteen, he ran into a series of misadventures, including killing a mutineer who attacked him.

Considered an expert in seamanship, Jones was pardoned but had to run from further problems and finally took a different name. After becoming an admiral and winning many sea battles for the colonies, he gained his most fame when he took on two British ships, the *Serapis* and *Countess of Scarborough*, which battered his ship perniciously.

After being asked by the British commander, "Do you ask for quarter (surrender)?" Jones replied, "I have not yet begun to fight!" This legendary cry inspired his crew to continue fighting to sink the two British ships, and became a hero in American history.

Barbarossa - (Roruk Aruj, d. 1518) was a pirate and marauder like his brother, Khayr ad-Din, but met an earlier death. He was a hearty fighter, changing sides whenever his moods or personal gains designated. He was killed by the Spaniards while helping Khayr ad-Din capture Algiers in 1518. Algiers was then added to the other Barbary States under the current Ottoman Empire. Earlier, he had fought for Spain as a privateer when the price was agreeable.

Barbarossa - (Khayr Ad Din, 1483-1546) Otherwise known as "Redbeard," Barbarossa was a powerful Ottoman admiral who defeated the Holy Roman Emperor, Charles V, at the Battle of Preveza in 1538. He also was a feared leader who fought against the Christians during their Crusades. Even though recognized as a pirate with his brother, Roruk, He was the Chief of the Ottoman Empire, and established a competent rule for his people, capturing most of Northern Africa as a base for his marauding ships.

Rob Roy - [Scottish Gaelic, - Red Rob], (1671-1734) Born Robert MacGregor, Rob Roy became a legend of Scotland for his brave fight to retain his land. Deprived of their estates, he and his highland clan lived by stealing cattle and championing the local populace. Sentenced in 1727 to be transported out of England, he was later pardoned. He is remembered in detail as the focus of Sir Walter Scott's novel *Rob Roy* (1818).

POLITICAL FIGURES

Armand Jean Richelieu - (1585-1642) Cardinal and Chief Minister to King Louis XIII of France from 1624-1642, the "Red Eminence" was a hardworking and conscientious man who was a major force in attaining an orderly government under royalty. He figured strongly in the building of artistic grandeur in France during that period.

Nell Gwynne - (1650-1687) Nell Eleanor was the popular English actress and mistress of Charles II. When she paid a visit to Oxford with the king one day, the crowd thought the king was with Louise de Kerouaille, his despised Roman Catholic mistress, and they began to shake his coach violently. Seeing the predicament and acting swiftly, Nell leaned out of the window of the coach and shouted, "Pray, good people, be civil, for I am the Protestant whore." She bore Charles two sons.

Rufus Matthew Jones - (1863-1948) A Quaker philosopher and leader who believed in a mystic interpretation of Christianity.

Harrison Grey Otis - (1765-1848) A gifted orator and leader in politics, he was a U.S. Senator from 1817 to 1822, and later became the first elected mayor of Boston.

Sir Winston Churchill - (1874-1965) Winston Churchill was a British statesman of undeterminable value to the strength and character of England during World War II. He was an excellent speaker and had a wonderful wit that endeared many to endure the hardships of war with a "stiff upper lip". Unfortunately, he was prone to "black" moods, or depressions, which caused him to be melancholy.

Once he asked a young woman, who had noticed him sitting at a table deep in thought, how old she was. She replied that she was nineteen. "And I," he replied sadly, "am thirty-two already." Then he commented angrily, "Curse ruthless time! Curse our mortality! How cruelly short is the allotted span for all we must cram into it!" He went into a dissertation about the brevity of life and stopped finally by saying, "We are all worms. But I do believe I am a glow worm."

Winston was cool, however, in matters of politics, and he rarely let others get his goat. He learned this by warding off jibes about his redhair in his youth, and figuring that most people who insulted others were trying too hard to be noticed.

Once, he was approached by a pompous American woman who asked rudely, "What are you going to do about those wretched Indians?"

"Madam," he answered, "to which Indians do you refer? Do you refer to the second greatest nation on earth (India), which under the benign and munificent British rule has multiplied and prospered exceedingly? Or to the unfortunate North American Indians, which under your present administration are almost extinct?"

Oliver Cromwell - (1599-1658) As the lord protector of England and a Puritan, Oliver Cromwell stood firmly with the opposition to Charles I. During the first civil war he gained leadership because of his military ability and genius for organization.

His regiment, the Ironsides, distinguished itself at Marston Moor in 1644 and in the following year he became second in command to Sir Thomas Fairfax in the New Model Army, which defeated King Charles at Naseby.

In the second civil war, he repelled the Scottish royalist invasion at Prestonin. He was prominent in demanding the execution of the king in 1649. After the republican Commonwealth was proclaimed, Cromwell led a cruel expedition into Ireland, where he tried to remove the Irish. Showing no mercy at times, he defeated the Scottish royalists at Dunbar in 1650, taking many of the prisoners and having them sold as indentured slaves to buyers in the English Colonies in America.

In 1653, the Protectorate was established and Cromwell was named lord protector. Even though he was eagerly offered the crown by his benefactors, he declined becoming a king for reasons unknown.

Opinions of Cromwell have always varied from good to bad, depending on whether you were English or Irish. He tolerated only Jews and non-Anglican Protestants, and unjustly created horrible conditions for the people of Ireland. He is recognized for his military genius but he practiced cruelty and intolerance when it came to dealing with the Irish. His son Richard Cromwell (1626-1712) succeeded him.

Rufus King - (1755-1827) American politician and diplomat, King was a member of the Continental Congress and served as ambassador to Great Britain from 1825 to 1826. (The name "rufus" in Latin pertains to "red").

Herbert Henry Asquith - (1852-1928) A British Prime Minister who introduced substantial social and constitutional changes in the British government. He was a Liberal, and remained head of the Liberal Party in England until 1926. He recounted a humorous incident that happened to him once while staying as a guest at the extremely rich Rothschild's estate. The butler, serving him at teatime, asked him his preference:

"Tea, coffee, or a peach from off the wall, sir?"

"Tea, please," Asquith said.

"China, Indian, or Ceylon?" the butler inquired.

"China, please."

"Lemon, milk, or cream, sir?" continued the butler.

"Milk, please," was Asquith's response.

"Jersey, Hereford, or Shorthorn, sir?"

Vladimir Lenin - (1870-1924) A Russian revolutionary writer who paired with Leon Trotsky, Lenin overthrew the czar and established communism as the form of government in Russia. He headed the Comintern government until his death. His doctrine is considered equal to Marx and Engels, and he once was looked upon as the father of his country by the Russian people. However, since the downfall of communism in the late 1980's, stories arose of his maniacal anger and methodical executions of tens of thousands of Russians, and he has been dishonored in the eyes of his people. In the fall of communism, Lenin's legacy of accomplishment was tarnished in the Soviet Union.

Jean Paul Marat - (1743-93) A French revolutionist, Marat was also a successful doctor and scientist. Both popular and disliked for his political views, he was responsible in part for several riots and massacres at political rallies that started the French Revolution.

Later, overcome by ill health, (he became sick after hiding in a sewer from an angry mob), he was stabbed to death in his bath by another redhead patriot, Charlotte Corday, who was upset at the human suffering that his actions caused.

Sulpicius Publius Rufus - (? - 88 B.C.) Orator in Rome during the century before Christ, Sulpicius was a friend and supporter of Marius and a tribune of the Plebes. He was executed when Sulla gained power.

William Lyon Mackenzie – (1795-1861) A Canadian journalist, reformer and politician, Mackenzie emigrated from his native Scotland to Upper Canada (now Ontario) in 1820. He founded the Colonial Advocate newspaper in 1824 and became a leader in the Reform party. He was elected to Upper Canada's legislature in 1828, but his constant attacks on the government led to his expulsion. Later, Mackenzie became Toronto's first mayor and then a legislator, helping to found the Constitution, an extreme organ of the Reform party, in 1836. In 1837, Mackenzie led a failed attempt aimed at capturing Toronto and overthrowing the government. He fled to the United States, and subsequently worked as a journalist and writer after becoming a U.S. citizen in 1843. He returned to Canada under an amnesty. In 1851, Mackenzie was once again reelected to the legislature, where he resumed his attacks on other political parties in power, until his resignation in 1858. He was a fiery tempered man but had a sense of humor. One story is that after he went bald from a fever, he began to wear a red wig which he would take off and wave around and hit his friends with in times of jest.

Marcus Caelius Rufus - (82 B.C. - 48 B.C.) A Roman politician and friend of Cicero, who after being accused of trying to kill his mistress, was defended by Cicero in one of his greatest oratories "Pro Caelius," which exonerated Caelius. Caelius was later killed, though, trying to overthrow Julius Caesar.

John Glenn - A U.S. astronaut and the first man in space, he later became a state senator and unsuccessfully ran for president in 1984.

Rufus Choate - (1799-1859) American politician who served as a U.S. representative and senator from

Massachusetts. He was recognized for his fierce idealistic politics in favor of the common man.

Lady Hamilton - (1765-1815) As Lord Nelson's mistress, Miss Hamilton was probably overrated in her supposed "eminent services" of procuring supplies and information for the British Fleet during the late 1790's. She had to eventually flee the country because of bad debts, even though her benefactor, Lord Nelson, had left her an ample financial trust when he died. She was a beautiful woman whose qualities were captured in hundreds of paintings by painters Romney, Gainsborough and Reynolds. Her hair was described as being "of the pure and perfect kind that goes with warm auburn hair."

Malcolm X, - Malcolm Little (1925-1965) An American Black activist, Malcolm was a member of the Black Muslims during 1952 to 1963. He was an idealistic proponent of separatism and pushed for unbridled Black pride. He converted to orthodox Islam, and founded the Organization of Afro-American Unity in 1964. Malcolm X was assassinated in Harlem while giving a speech.

Rufus Wheeler Peckham - (1838-1909) American judge (jurist) who served as an associate justice of the U.S. Supreme Court from 1896 to 1909.

Lynette "Squeaky" Fromme - A cult follower of convicted mass murderer Charles Manson, Fromme fired several shots from a pistol in her assassination attempt on U.S. President Gerald Ford in 1975. She purportedly was letting off steam after being kicked out of her house by her father. Fromme had previously served half of a ten year sentence for her involvement in the infamous Manson murders of actress Sharon Tate and others.

U.S. PRESIDENTS

George Washington - (1732-1799) As most Americans know, George Washington was a general and the first President of the United States of America. The leader of the American troops during the Revolutionary War, he gained legendary respect from his countrymen, earning him much power during the formation of the new U.S. government. He was known as a "soldier's general" by getting into the midst of battle and experiencing the woes of war next to his men.

Once, while riding through his ranks during the bitter cold at Valley Forge, he came across a revolutionary soldier drinking some stolen wine. Slightly drunk already, the young man gladly asked his commander to "drink some wine with a soldier." But Washington told him it was not the right time to be drinking wine.

"Damn you," the tipsy soldier cried out, "you're above drinking with us!"

Washington turned around and said, "Come, I will drink with you," and took a swig from the bottle and handed it back. The young soldier held it out again and said, "Give some to your servants." As Washington's aides passed the bottle around, the soldier proudly stated, "I'll be damned if I don't spend the last drop of my blood for you."

Thomas Jefferson - (1743-1826) Chief author of the Declaration of Independence and 3rd President of the United States. Jefferson, nicknamed "The Red

Fox," was capably talented in art and music and was a renowned scholar.

When Jefferson was visited by the Baron von Humboldt, the German scientist and explorer, the baron found a newspaper in Jefferson's presidential office containing abusive remarks about Jefferson.

"Why is this libelous journal not suppressed?" asked the Baron. "Or why do you not fine the editor, or imprison him?"

Jefferson smiled at his guest and replied, "Put that paper in your pocket, Baron, and if you hear the reality of our liberty, the freedom of the press questioned, show them this paper and tell them where you found it."

A man of great words and philosophies, Jefferson once said in a letter to Benjamin Rush in 1803, "It behooves every man who values liberty of conscience for himself to resist invasions of it in the case of others."

In another letter to S. Kercheval in 1810, Jefferson wrote, "But a short time elapsed after the death of the great reformer of the Jewish religion (Jesus Christ), before His principles were departed from by those who professed to be His special servants, and perverted into an engine for enslaving mankind, and aggrandizing their oppressors in Church and State."

Martin Van Buren - (1782-1862) As the 8th President of the United States, Martin Van Buren was the first president that was born a citizen of the United States and not born under British rule. Not happy about inheriting the economic problems of his predecessor, Andrew Jackson, Van Buren was glad to retire to his farm after his term in office. He was despised by the states of the South, and actually received only nine popular votes in his election from that area. His supporters, though, cried fraud.

"Yes, fraud," said a Virginian, "and we are still looking for the s--o--b who voted nine times."

Ulysses S. Grant - (1822-1885) 18th President of the United States, Grant was a feared and able general in the American Civil War where he became the commander of the Union Army. Accused and probably guilty of being a heavy drinker, he was still a competent and capable soldier who earned the respect of Abraham Lincoln, who once said, "If I knew of the brand of whiskey he drank, I would send it to all my generals!"

General Grant was not a sharp dresser by nature, and once, while staying at an inn on a wet stormy night, he wandered into the lobby where there was a group of lawyers gathered around the fire. One looked at him and said, "Here's a stranger, gentleman, and by the looks of him he's traveled through hell itself to get here."

"That's right," said Grant amiably.

"And how did you find things down there?"

"Just like here," replied Grant, "the lawyers all closest to the fire."

Andrew Jackson - (1767-1845) The 7th President of the United States and a decorated military hero,

Andrew Jackson was nicknamed "Old Hickory" for several reasons; he was tall and wiry, and he stood strong in his convictions and actions.

Jackson began his reputation as a fearless lawmaker when as a presiding judge in a small town, he encountered a notorious ruffian by the name of Russell Bean. As Bean created a ruckus outside of the courthouse, several men tried to arrest him, including the sheriff, but no man had the desire to collar him because Bean was swearing that he would shoot anyone who came near him. Seeing the commotion, Jackson grabbed his pistols and worked his way through the crowd to Bean.

Face to face with the man, Jackson ordered, "Surrender this instant, or I'll blow you through!" Bean, stunned by Jackson's forcefulness, eyed him a moment, and then sheepishly submitted to be led away. Asked why he had given up so easily to Jackson, Bean replied, "When he came up I looked him in the eye, and I saw "shoot," and there wasn't any "shoot" in nary another eye in the crowd; so I says to myself, says I, 'hoss, it's about time to sing small,' and so I did."

Calvin Coolidge - (1872-1933) As the 30th President of the United States, Calvin Coolidge was a hard-working, studious, but quiet man. He was well-respected as President and was deemed an efficient administrator who got the job done. After two successful terms, he declined to run again for office despite his continuing popularity, and he is considered to have been one of the most honest leaders in American politics.

Called "Red" in his youth, his hair began to turn a shade browner as he got older, and they began calling him "Silent Cal" for his lack of desire to engage in petty conversation. Once, at a dinner party, a wife of a senator turned to him and said, "I bet I can get you to say three words."

"You lost," he quickly responded.

Dwight David Eisenhower - (1890-1969), American general and 34th president of the U.S. (1953-61), Dwight Eisenhower was called "Ike" by most, but in West Point, he was called "Red Ike." Eisenhower had an explosive rise as a military commander during WW II. In 1942 he became chief of army operations in Washington, D.C. and soon after he was named U.S. commander of the European Allied troops. Eisenhower coordinated and directed the Allied invasion of Europe in June 1944. He organized the troops of the North Atlantic Treaty Organization (NATO), but then resigned from the army to campaign for the Republican presidential nomination. Being a war hero gave him an easy election victory over his rival, Democratic opponent, Adlai E. Stevenson. During his term, Eisenhower remained aloof from the legislative process and introduced few initiatives. Despite a heart attack in 1955 he easily won re-election in 1956. He was very supportive of the civil rights movement during this period. In 1957 Eisenhower sent federal troops to Little Rock, Arkansas to enforce a court-ordered school desegregation order. He was known to be tough, but sensitive to populous issues.

ROYALTY

Cleopatra - (69 - 30 B.C.) As the Queen of Egypt, Cleopatra was both extremely smart and seductive, using her beauty and alluring nature to capture an empire for herself. She seduced Julius Caesar by throwing herself at his feet when he came with a small army to war with Egypt. Instead of taking over Egypt for himself, Caesar withdrew his troops and gave Egypt to her which she ruled for over a decade. Cleopatra was mad that he didn't divorce his Roman wife, but after Caesar was killed, she decided to stay out of Rome and not make any royal claims for herself. She then met the Roman commander Marc Antony and seduced him into letting her keep her rule in Egypt.

When Caesar's heir, Octavion, became fed up with Antony's indiscretions with Cleopatra, he attacked him with his armies. Marc Antony committed suicide when his last stronghold at Alexandria was breached. Distraught after being captured by Octavion, Cleopatra desired to join Antony in death, although Octavion wished her alive. She allowed herself to be bit by an asp that a friend had brought to her hidden in a basket of figs and she died shortly after.

Her beauty was legend, and adding the red to her hair (See "Henna") just made her more outstanding to her subjects. Truly a woman of destiny, she lived a fast and luxurious life with two of the most powerful men of her time.

Henry II - (1133-89) Henry became King of England after his mother, Matilda, who was the daughter of Henry I, convinced her cousin Stephen to adopt him as his next heir. Stephen, who had seized the English throne upon Henry I's death, yielded the throne sooner when Henry II arrived with his armies. As the new king, Henry II was instrumental in forming a more centralized and unified government, dominating the old structure of feudal aristocracy.

In a story of heartbreak and irony, he appointed his good friend Thomas á Becket to chancellor in 1154 and then to Archbishop of Canterbury in 1162, hoping to unite the church and the state. Becket rebelled and refused to give Henry II control to the church. In a rage, Henry cried out, "What a parcel of fools and dastards have I nourished in my house that not one of them will avenge me of this upstart clerk (Becket)!"

Four of his knights took the King literally and killed Becket at the alter of Canterbury Cathedral. Becket's death devastated Henry II, and he anguished over it until his own death.

Queen Elizabeth I - (1533-1603), Queen of England and Ireland from 1558 to 1603, Elizabeth was the daughter of Henry VIII and Anne Boleyn. One of her most important accomplishments was establishing England as a dominant naval power when she attained major victories over the Spanish Armada, at that time considered the most formidable navy in the world. On a darker note, some historians believe she had her cousin, Mary, Queen of Scots, beheaded for treason, but otherwise she was a commendable Monarch.

Considered the most powerful woman who has ever lived, she was a personality who encouraged her court to dote on her, and was a fancier of handsome and heroic men, such as Sir Walter Raleigh.

The English court during her rule became the most elegant in its history. Although considered unattractive, she was a very intelligent, yet fair and merciful woman who once gestured a knight in ill-favor with the court to rise after he threw himself at her feet for mercy. He had previously treated her disrespectfully when she was in obscurity while her half-sister Mary was ruler. She bade the knight a dismissal of his actions by saying, "Do you not know that we are descended of the lion, whose nature is not to prey upon the mouse or any other such small vermin?"

Henry VIII - (1491-1547) As King of England, his first wife could not bear him a male heir, which forced him for political reasons to disengage the papal authority from the Roman Church, and to form the Anglican Church. Henry VIII was a tyrant, but also a strong ruler for England, and he established his country as a formidable European power. A horrible husband, he was also known for executing several of his wives, including Anne Boleyn, the mother of Elizabeth I.

In one incident, he was encouraged by his minister, Thomas Cromwell, to marry a Flemish princess, Anne of Cleves, in order to strengthen ties with Protestant Europe. A painter had provided a beautiful portrait of the King's bride, (he had not met her yet) which made him look forward to meeting her. She turned out to be less desirable than her picture depicted.

"You have sent me a Flanders mare," the King complained disgustedly. Shortly thereafter, he had Cromwell executed on a trumped-up charge of treason.

William the Conqueror - (1027-1087) Before William became the King of England, he was the Duke of Normandy with a poor hold on the ascent to the English throne. He set out with his Norman troops to take over the English monarchy, and at one point, when he tripped and fell while invading the shore of England, his superstitious men quivered at what they considered a bad omen. But William, grabbing sand in his hands, quickly jumped up and cried, "By the splendor of God I have taken possession of my realm – the earth of England is in my two hands."

He killed his rival to the throne, King Harold, in one of history's greatest conflicts, the Battle of Hastings, and took over as ruler of England. As King, he blended the Normans and the Saxons into one country, a move of strength that permanently made England a great power. His Norse vigor was mixed into the decaying Saxon hierarchy and he rebuilt the English land, keeping a "Domesday" book listing all property owned in the country down to the minutest detail. He is considered one of the greatest English rulers in history, and important in the formation of European politics.

Being a hotheaded redhead, he went on a war party against France on a jest by its king about his portly figure. After riding through the ruins of a French town, William's horse tripped and fell upon him, gravely injuring him, and he died several weeks later. His second son, William Rufus, another redhead, became the next King of England.

Frederick Barbarossa - (1123-1190) A twelfth century King of Germany, Frederick was idolized by his people and considered an honorable man and a good ruler by the standards of his day. He became the sovereign ruler of the feudal territories of the Holy Roman Empire in 1183.

His namesake "Barbarossa" actually meant "redbeard", a sobriquet that he relished. His subjects used to proclaim "Here comes the Sunset!" when they saw him coming. Even though they joked about the King's majestic redhair, he never punished them for it, for he knew they looked at his colorful markings as a "red badge of courage". His bravery was legendary even in his lifetime, but sadly, he drowned in the Saleph River while leading his armies during the Crusades.

Queen Alexandra - (1844-1925) A Danish princess, Alexandra married the Prince of Wales, the man who later became King Edward the VII of Great Britain. She put up with his infidelities and hedonistic desires throughout their marriage, and suffered through it acting as if she knew nothing. When the King died, she was grief-stricken, but her sense of humor quickly returned.

"Now at least I know where he is," she commented to her friend Lord Esher.

Princess Victoria – She was the daughter of Liliuokalani, the last Queen of Hawaii. Considered a extremely beautiful woman, Princess Victoria had a four-foot mane of dark redhair.

Mary, Queen of Scots - (1542-1587) Mary became Queen of Scotland shortly after her birth and her mother acted as regent. She grew up in the French court, and married a Dauphin (who later became Francis II), and upon his death, she returned to Scotland. She married her second husband's murderer, the Earl of Bothwell, and the Scottish nobles rebelled. She fled the country, and was held captive by another redhead, Queen Elizabeth I.

Mary had long laid claim to the Queen of England's throne, but Elizabeth had her executed for treason. Upon her beheading, the executioner picked Mary's head up by her beautiful red hair, for which she had always been admired, so he could show the crowd (this was customary), and discovered he was holding onto a wig attached to a handkerchief. He looked down at her severed head and saw she was almost completely bald.

Maire Ruadh (Red Maire) - Maire was an Irish queen who allegedly ridded herself of her unwanted husbands by having them blindfolded and then thrown from her castle window down to the rocks of the Ariantic shores below. There seems to be little information available about this person.

Catherine the Great - (1729-1796) As Empress of Russia, Catherine first married the future Czar, Peter III, who treated her unkindly and embarrassed her often. He was later deposed and killed. She succeeded him at the throne, and was considered a promiscuous woman with many advisors who were also her lovers. A daring and courageous leader, however, she expanded Russian territory with wars against the Turks and Poland. She was also very influenced by the Western culture, and regularly entertained the famous personalities of Europe in her court.

Sarah Ferguson - "Prince Andrew To Wed Redheaded Commoner" blared the headlines in the Los Angeles Times on March 20, 1986. Nicknamed "Fergie," Sarah Ferguson is the daughter of Prince Charles' polo manager, retired army Maj. Ronald Ferguson. Born in 1960, Sarah's family has been closely linked with British royalty, and she is descended from King Charles II. After her marriage to Prince Andrew, she became the Duchess of York. Prince Andrew, when asked what he liked about her, replied, "Wit, charm, and the red hair." Their marriage was the event of the year in 1986. They separated six years later in 1992.

King William Rufus - The second son of William the Conqueror, Rufus was a disliked monarch during his rule from 1087 to 1100 A.D. A large and stocky man, he had an "evil eye" and redhair with a reddish complexion that turned redder as he became angry.

A pursuer of a great many vices, he was looked upon by many of his subjects with scorn. He was killed by an arrow from a crossbow while on a hunting excursion, allegedly by Walter Tyrell, who steadfastly denied it, but who still had to flee to France to protect his own life. William Rufus was buried by a charcoal carrier without any religious ceremonies, as it was considered sacrilegious in those days to give a holy ceremony to a known evil or sinful man.

Rurik of Novgorod - A Danish Viking leader, Rurik, along with his Varangian tribes, settled in the Eastern Slavic countries and established the first Russian state of Kiev which he ruled from 862 - 879 A.D. He was a bold and powerful man, and the Slavic people sought him to become their leader to protect them from other European nations and the Mongols that were enslaving their Serbian populations. Ruler of the Rus (roos) Dynasty, which remained in power for over 700 years, Rurik's name meant "redhaired King" and the name "Rus" loosely meant "of the reddish-haired people," an apt description of him and his Viking settlers, being that they were fairer-skinned and lighter-haired than most of the Slavic people. From the Rus Dynasty comes the present day name "Russia," basically meaning "Land of the reddish people." (See "Translations")

Hugh O'Neill - An Irish general who was respected by his enemies as a brave and worthy opponent, O'Neill led his armies against Oliver Cromwell of England. He was captured, though, after a long and bloody battle, but was spared and imprisoned until his release two years later when they allowed him to go to Spain. There he wrote to King Charles and requested his earldom as the 2nd Earl of Tyrone, and died never returning to the British Isles.

Gilbert de Clare, Earl of Gloucester - (1243-1295) Called the "Red Earl," Gilbert de Clare was a Welsh nobleman during King Henry III's reign. He married the King's niece, Alice of Angouleme, and became a member of the baronial party led by Simon de Montfort. The barons joined together and fought against the King at the Battle of Lewes in 1264, and the King surrendered to the Montfort. Gloucester quarreled with Montfort, though, and decided to return to his Welsh homelands, where he met Prince Edward (later Edward I) and helped him in victory at Evesham in 1265. He eventually gained favor with King Henry III and Prince Edward by allying the barons to the King, which was the major force behind the collapse of the baronial party.

Sir John Comyn the Younger - Nephew of King John of Scotland, "Red Comyn" was stabbed to death in a church because of a feud with another redhead, Robert Bruce, in 1306.

Hugh O'Donnell - (1572-1602) The last of the old Gaelic Kings that ruled Ireland, Hugh O'Donnell by the age of twenty was a chieftain of the O'Donnell clan and a major foe of the English from previous excursions against them. He formed his hatred for the English when he was kidnapped at age sixteen by Sir John Perrot, the English Lord Deputy, who was afraid of the O'Neills and O'Donnell's organizing against him.

Secured within the Dublin castle dungeon, "Red Hugh" escaped after his second year and later led his men on a series of attacks to secure Ireland from scattered English lords. His most remarkable feat was covering 40 miles through the Slieve Phelim Mountains in 24 hours to meet up with Tyrone at the battle of Kinsdale. His mistake of supporting the Spanish commander to attack immediately was probably the beginning of the major defeat that forced him to leave Ireland and settle in Spain, where he died, supposedly poisoned by an English agent.

INNOVATORS & PIONEERS

Walter Reuther - (1907-1970) Pioneer of the birth of the Labor Union in the United States, Walter Reuther (nicknamed "The Red-headed Kid From Wheeling") served as the head of the United Auto Workers and became president of the Congress of Industrial Organizations.

Once, as Reuther visited an auto factory, a young executive gushed out his enthusiasm for a new process they had for robotizing the assembly line. He went on non-stop about the benefits of robotics when Reuther interrupted, "And tell me, sir, these new robots - will they go out and buy the cars from your company?"

Robert Ingersoll - (1833-1899) A freethinker, Ingersoll travelled the country intelligently lambasting religion and what he perceived as illogical thinking in the organized dogma of Christianity. His ideas on philosophy and goodwill towards others helped expand intellectual thought and contributed to the Age of Enlightenment. Ingersoll's personal belief was simple, yet agreeable: "I have a creed: happiness is the only good; the way to be happy is to make others so; the place to be happy is here; and the time to be happy is now!"

Tycho Brahe - (1546-1601) As a Danish astronomer, Brahe broke through the current beliefs that the heavens were fixed when he provided evidence showing planetary motion. At the young age of 26, Brahe viewed a supernova and verified it as a new star. He was a key figure in the start of modern astronomy, and is under-rated as a prominent scientist during his time period.

Solomon Schechter - (1847-1915) A highly esteemed rabbi and scholar, Schechter became president of the Jewish Theological Seminary of America from 1902 until his death. In 1896, he was the person responsible for finding the original manuscripts for the Hebrew version of *Ecclesiasticus*. His work was primary in helping to establish conservative Jewish viewpoints along more traditional interpretations of the Bible.

Lela Secor - (1887-1966) A journalist and feminist, in 1915 Secor sailed on the Ford Peace Expedition to Europe. That effort, though futile, inspired her to commit her life to the pursuit of world peace. She was member of the American Neutral Conference Committee and the Emergency Peace Federation.

Margaret Sanger - (1879-1966) Born Margaret Louise Higgins, she attributed her mother's tuberculosis and the family's lack of financial security to the fact that her parents had too many children. Margaret always felt that her mother died prematurely at forty-nine because of the hardship of trying to support her and her ten brothers and sisters. Her father, Michael, was a freethinker who avoided work often in favor of espousing his political viewpoints.

Encouraged by her father's rebelliousness, she went on to buck the popular beliefs towards women's rights (little existed at that time) and became a leader of modern birth control efforts. After marrying William Sanger and learning about birth firsthand, she became a pioneer of women's rights concerning their bodies, basing much of her convictions on her personal tragedies because of unwanted or unneeded births. She is considered one of the great woman social leaders of this century.

L. Ron Hubbard - (1911-1985) U.S. science fiction writer and founder of the Church of Scientology, L. (Lafayette) Ronald Hubbard based the tenets of his church on his best-selling 1950 book *Dianetics - The Modern Science of Mental Health*. Hubbard believed that man is essentially a free and immortal spirit who can achieve his true nature only by freeing himself of emotional encumbrances of the past through counseling ("auditing"). His "applied religious philosophy" made him a fortune, but British authorities in 1968 refused entry to Scientology students and teachers on the grounds that Scientology is "socially harmful" and stated that its "authoritarian principles and practices are a potential menace to the well-being of those so deluded as to become followers." He was constantly plagued with infighting and ridicule, and he died amid controversy, but his book *Dianetics* continues to be a perennial bestseller.

Paul "Red" Adair - When Paul Adair developed successful techniques to quell oil fires, his company became considered the best oil firefighting crew in the world, and was hired to put out the thousands of well fires set by retreating Iraqis in the Desert Storm War.

Galileo - (1564-1642) At the young age of 19, Galileo discovered *isochronism,* a principle proving that a pendulum swings the same amount of times in a given period despite changes of amplitude. He was a mathematician, astronomer, and physicist who was best recognized for designing the telescope with which he discovered moons around Jupiter. He was also known for proposing that two bodies do not fall at the speed proportional to their weight. The latter discovery was not met with acceptance because it belied the teachings of Aristotle. Galileo made other scientific discoveries and pushed the belief of the Copernican System of astronomy, which changed the current way of thinking in scientific and philosophical arenas. He was brought before the Inquisition and forced to renounce his theories concerning the Copernican system.

Discovering the parabola (path of a projectile), Galileo also was credited with studies leading to Sir Isaac Newton's discovery of the law of gravity.

Marion Ross – actress (Mrs. Cunningham in "Happy Days" television series)

Chapter Two

ARTS

Redheads have contributed greatly to the arts, especially in the field of writing, but in every field, one or more redheads have been the pioneer or leader in discovery or changes in their respective areas. Youthful alienation, redhead hyperactivity, superior intellect, and early thrusts toward individuality have made these men and women excel in setting the standards to which others have respected or followed throughout the years.

MUSIC

Ignace Jan Paderewski - (1860-1941) A Polish piano virtuoso and statesman, Paderewski became Prime Minister of Poland in 1919, but could not bring unity to the country so he resigned. When he played before Queen Victoria, she exclaimed that he was a genius. As he always talked about the amount of hours he practiced, he replied to Her Highness, "Perhaps I am a genius, Your Majesty, but before that I was a drudge."

Antonio Vivaldi - (1669-1741) An Italian composer and violinist, Vivaldi is best-known for carrying the concerto form to its highest stage of development in technique and expression. He wrote the "Gloria," one of the most sublime works ever composed for the human voice. Known as the "Red Priest," because of his priesthood and redhair, his most popular works, "The Four Seasons," is a moving and brilliant expression of musical ideas that signify the changing of the seasons in the year. Johann Sebastian Bach was greatly influenced, as were many other famous composers, by Vivaldi's compositions and style. Bach was intrigued with Vivaldi's talents and probably styled his own material to follow Vivaldi's precedent.

Ginger Baker - Tall redheaded and redbearded drummer, Baker played for the 1960's innovative rock bands "Cream" and "Blind Faith." Both were English bands that featured cutting edge vocal and guitar styles during that time. The band Blind Faith also consisted of guitarist Eric Clapton and vocalist Stevie Winwood.

Mick Hucknall - An almost sopranic singer, Hucknall is the leader of the soulful pop band, Simply Red. First gaining popularity in the mid 1980's, their debut album, "Picture Book" scored with two top 20 hits, "Holding Back the Years," and "Money's too Tight to Mention."

Red Holloway - A blues and jazz aficionado, Red Holloway is considered one of the present day's foremost saxophonist. Playing with such greats as Dizzy Gillespie, Carmen McRae, and George Benson, Holloway secured a place in the Jazz Hall of Fame during his lifetime with his high-styled but soulful musical techniques.

Jonathan Waite - Pop rock singer who first sang with the band, The Babys, in the late 1970's, Waite went on to more fame in a solo career with his hit, "Missing You," in 1984.

Danny Elfman - Avant garde musician and singer with the 1980's band Oingo Boingo, Elfman also has also done the musical scores for many popular movies and television shows, including "Tales From The Crypt." His trademark style is known for its expressively quirky melodies and beats.

BrickTop – Female blues singer who had her own nightclub in the 1930's and was written about by author Ernest Hemingway.

Red Narva – Considered the Virtuoso of Vibraphone, Red is an accomplished player of the xylophone and the marimba. He recorded music at the Smithsonian in his seventies.

Bonnie Raitt - One of the top blues pop singers in the country, Bonnie has earned eight Grammy Awards in her 25 years of writing and performing music. Known for her love of playing for live audiences, she blends a blues sensibility with an evocative singing style and eloquent slide guitar. "Nick of Time" and "Luck of the Draw," are two of her top-selling albums. She was born in Burbank, California.

Johann Strauss the Younger - A composer famous for his Viennese waltzes and operettas, Strauss actually fooled his father, who didn't want him to be a musician, into thinking he was a clerk while secretly practicing on his violin. After his father's death, he traveled to Russia and England and won acclaim along with many fans for his music. His most famous composition is "The Blue Danube," one of the most recognized works in the world today, as it was in his day. He wrote over 500 dance pieces and orchestrations, becoming one of the most listened to composers of the 19th Century.

The Judds - Popular redhaired mother and daughter country singing duo, Naomi and Wynnona Judd (mother and daughter respectively) have won several awards for their songs, including an American Music Award and a Grammy for their song "Grandpa" in 1987.

When asked about becoming an honorary member of the club, Redheads International, Wynnona accepted, saying "We redheads have to stick together."

Tori Amos - Considered one of alternative music's most strongly confident singers, Tori's songs carry a cynicism and wit that reflect her life growing up as a redhead. She was trained as a classical pianist.

PAINTERS

Titian - (1488-1576) A famous Italian painter, Titian's paintings featured so many women displaying hair of deep red, that today his name "Titian" is used to signify that particular color. During his lifetime, because he popularized his redhaired models through his paintings, women were dyeing their hair with soda, alum, sulfur and seawater to try to capture the look that the women in his paintings characterized.

The Duchess of Urbino, even though she was quite unattractive and along in years, had asked her husband to commission Titian to paint her in the nude. Titian was far from enthusiastic about the job, but his friend, the satirist and poet Pietro Aretino, found a solution. They hired a beautiful and shapely prostitute to pose for the figure, and Titian glossed a generous portrait of the duchess's face on top of the body modeled by the prostitute.

The duchess was overjoyed by the painting, but her husband sighed, "If I could have had that girl's body, even with my wife's head, I would have been a happier man." Aretino, when he heard this, broke out in such hysterical laughter that he suffered a stroke and keeled over dead.

Vincent Van Gogh - (1853-1890) A Dutch painter, Van Gogh is recognized as a pioneer in the use of brilliant swirling colors and abstract perspective in painting. His later works are considered among the most influential of modern art. Dropping out of several art schools because of his moody disposition (mostly caused by his misfortunes with women, one being a French prostitute who he sent his self-amputated ear), he finally settled down in Aries, France, where he painted hundreds of portraits and landscapes. His most famous is *Starry Night*. Committing himself to an institution for bouts of depression, he sometimes did his best work during these periods. Finally, at the end of his most prominent three years of works, he shot and killed himself.

Red Grooms - Famous contemporary artist and painter, Grooms excels in absurd and abstract statements with his art. He pioneered a new art form called "the happening," and is best-known for his clever environmental constructions. A popular artist of the 20th century, his works are considered very valuable as collectors art, a rare feat during an artist's lifetime.

Victorine Meureut - Although Ms. Meureut was not a painter, she was the favorite model of painter Edouard Manet. She appeared in many of his famous paintings, including the whimsical "Gare St. Lazare," which proudly shows her beautiful flowing redhair.

AUTHORS, WRITERS & POETS

Mark Twain - (1835-1910) Born Samuel Langhorne Clemens, he was an American author, humorist and lecturer. He engaged in a myriad of occupations, all of them having a certain adventurous excitement to them. His most popular works, "Tom Sawyer" and "Huckleberry Finn" are considered American classics without peer.

One of America's most beloved wits, he wrote a series of short stories that reflected the ironies and subtleties of the human condition and is considered a mirror of late 19th century American and European attitudes. A popular speaker, he nevertheless died without attaining any real fortune, and was constantly trying to keep out of debt during his life.

A regular and unabashed cigar smoker, Twain disliked anyone who made a complaint against smoking. To those who asked him if it was hard for him to quit smoking, he would reply, "It's easy, I've done it a hundred times!"

Twain was an irrepressible rascal and loved to brag about his fishing and hunting trips. As he was returning from a fishing excursion in Maine, despite that the fishing season was closed at the time, he looked for someone in his lounge car to whom he could tell his tall tales. Settling on a stranger, he began bragging of the massive fish that he had caught. After viewing the distasteful look on the stranger's face, Twain asked him who he was, and whether he like to fish. The stranger replied, "I'm the state game warden, who are you?" Seeing the trouble he had made for himself, Twain quickly said, "Well, to be perfectly truthful, warden, I'm the biggest damn liar in the whole United States!"

Algernon Charles Swinburne - (1837-1909) A famous English poet and critic, Algernon Swinburne was a scandalous character in the repressed morality of the Victorian period of his day. His volume of works "Poems and Ballads" was a parody and defiant celebration of a casual sexual attitude.

Swinburne had it hard at his school. One of his old school chum's recalled at a party: "When the head-boy at Eton called all of us together, he pointed to a little fellow with a mass of curly redhair and said, 'If you ever see that boy, kick him, and if you are too far off to kick him, throw a stone at him.' I remember it was a boy named Swinburne and he used to write poetry, but I don't know what became of him."

James Joyce - (1882-1941) An Irish novelist, he is bestknown for his masterpiece "Ulysses," and novels "Finnegans Wake," and "A Portrait of the Artist as a Young Man." He left Ireland in 1902 and spent the rest of his days in America collaborating with other great writers such as Pound and Frost.

Once, while applying for a job in a bank, the bank manager asked him several questions:

"Do you smoke?"

"No, "replied Joyce.

"Do you drink?"

"No."

"Do you go out with any girls?" the manager continued questioning.

"Not often," was the final reply from Joyce. The bank manager was not impressed by Joyce's seemingly virtuous character and thought him odd.

"Away with you!" the manager cried. "You'd probably rob the bank!"

In another incidence, Joyce was asked about what he demands of his readers, he replied, "The demand I make of my readers is that they devote their whole life to reading my works."

William Blake - (1757-1827) An English artist and poet, Blake's works had a prominent mysticism that were little understood during his day. Some of his more known books include, "Songs of Innocence" (1789), and "Jerusalem" (1808-18). He also illustrated books for other authors, among them being Dante's "Divina Commedia" (Divine Comedy). His believed task was to "open the mortal eyes of Man inward into the Worlds of Thought." An artistic visionary and genius, Blake always credited his works to some divine direction.

Known to see visions even in early childhood, he refused an apprenticeship with William Ryland, a well-respected engraver, because the man had the face that "looked like he will live to be hanged." Blake's father, somewhat astounded, relinquished the arrangement in his boy's favor, and set him up as an apprentice to a little-known engraver, James Basire. Many years later, the first engraver, Ryland, went bankrupt after the failure of his business and had committed a forgery. He was later caught, convicted - and hanged.

Jean Paul Sartre - (1905 - 1980) A French philosopher and novelist, Sartre wrote several books dealing with the meaning of life, including "Nausea," and "The Age of Reason." The founder of the thought that all philosophy should begin with the focus on the "meaninglessness of existence," Sartre is considered the leader of the philosophy in existentialism. (See "Red Quips")

Sinclair Lewis - (1885-1951) An American novelist, Lewis' books, "Babbitt" and "Main Street," were social satires on Middle America that are standards today, although considered controversial in the 1920's when they were first published. His later days as a dramatist were not as successful, though, and he returned to writing and lecturing.

Booked as a lecturer at Columbia University for a speech to student writers, Lewis began by asking them, "How many of you here are really serious about being writers?" The room was filled immediately with raised hands. "Well, why the hell aren't you all home writing?" he said, and sat down.

William Shakespeare - (1564-1616) An English poet and playwright, Shakespeare is recognized as the greatest writer of plays in history. Many of his plays were performed at the Globe Theatre in London, and included comedies "Much Ado about Nothing" and "As You Like It," and tragedies, such as "Hamlet," "Othello", and "King Lear." He also wrote historical works, such as "Richard II." The earliest collection of his plays, *The First Folio*, contained 36 plays and was published after his death in 1623. He also composed 154 sonnets.

It was said that William Shakespeare was born at Stratford-upon-Avon in the county of Warwick and his father was a butcher. Legend has it when Shakespeare was a boy, he worked along side his father, but when he killed a calf, he would do it in a high style and make a speech eulogizing the animal.

George Bernard Shaw - (1856-1950) An Irish playwright and successful music and drama critic Shaw's works are still popular and revered for their biting wit. His criticism is still considered brilliant in intellectual circles and in 1925 he was awarded the Nobel Prize for literature. A Fabian socialist, Shaw was a popular speaker and believed that poverty was the source of all evil.

Before Shaw had become famous, one of his plays was turned down time after time by a particular producer. After Shaw had become popular, the same producer offered to stage Shaw's work that he had earlier rejected. Shaw wrote him back and said, "Better never than late."

Once, while Shaw was a music critic, he dined with a friend at a restaurant that featured an orchestra that was not quite up to par. The leader asked him what he would like the orchestra to play next, and Shaw replied, "Dominoes."

Shaw during his life was so respected in the performing arts that when he died, most theaters around the world stayed dark for a day in his honor.

D.H. Lawrence - (1885-1930) Born David Herbert Lawrence, he became a renowned British novelist and poet, whose book "Sons and Lovers" caused a scandal for its sexual explicitness and the fact that it was fashioned mostly from his own youthful experiences. He spent much of his life traveling, writing down the details of his amorous adventures.

Most of his books were considered racy, and one of his best-known novels, "Lady Chatterly's Lover" was not printed in its unexpurgated form until 1961, many years after his death. His writing, lyrical and sensuous, was considered brilliant and influenced the writings of the 20th century. His first novel, "The White Peacock", was published in 1911. He gave his mother a copy while she was near death, and his father, a miner, struggled through half a page. He asked his son how much he was paid for the book, and Lawrence replied "Fifty pounds, father." His father was amazed and said, "Fifty pounds! An' tha's niver done a day's hard work in thy life!"

Evelyn Waugh - (1903-1966) A British novelist, Waugh penned "Decline and Fall" and "Brideshead Revisited". Also known as Arthur St. John, he wrote a wartime trilogy, "At Arms", "Officers and Gentlemen", and "Unconditional Surrender". He was a social satirist highly recognized during his lifetime for his wit and insight supporting moral conservatism.

Known for his courage in battle during the fighting on the island of Crete in 1941, his commander asked Waugh what were his first impressions of military action.

"Like German opera," replied Waugh, "too long and too loud."

Emily Dickinson - (1830-1886) Called the "New England Mystic" she was a poet who experimented with rhymes and rhythms, creating interesting webs of grammatical turns and paths. Almost all of her work was misunderstood in her time, and was published mostly after her death. Pushed into religious doctrinations in her early life, she had strong feelings about God, but remained a skeptic, which created tension in many of her spiritual poems.

She was a recluse in the home of her birthplace in Amherst, Massachusetts home, where she wrote over one thousand poems during the Civil War period. She is recognized today as one of the most intriguing and intelligent American writers who have ever lived.

Dissent

Assent - and you are sane,
Demur - you're straightway dangerous,
And handled with a Chain.
Emily Dickinson

Tom Robbins - The author of "Still Life With Woodpecker," Robbins also wrote "Even Cowgirls Get the Blues," an odd fictional tale of two redhaired lovers. In one of his books, a blonde character states "Red hair is caused by sugar and lust. Highly evolved beings do not indulge in sugar and lust."
(See "Characters")

Ezra Pound - (1885-1972) An American poet who was the major force in the growth and influencing of English literature in the 20th Century, Pound was referred to as the "Poet's poet." He was among the first men to recognize the writing talents of James Joyce, D.H. Lawrence, and Robert Frost. He served as the editor on many respected literary magazines, and contributed to other articles by famous authors, such as his friend, Irish poet and playwright, William Yeats. He moved to Italy and helped develop economic theories that caused him to read broadcasts of fascist propaganda during World War II. After the war, he was arrested for treason and was confined to a mental hospital until 1958. He published over 70 books in his lifetime and more than 1,500 separate articles, including "The Cantos," which took 35 years to finish.

Rupert Brooke - (1887-1915) An English poet, Brooke was very popular in his days as a handsome, gifted young man. A distinguished scholar and celebrated as a talented cricket and football player, he earned a multitude of friends and admirers. He was heavily romanticized in biographies after his untimely and early death on a hospital ship returning from a disastrous expedition to Antwerp during WW I. He became famous during the war for his poems that intimated romantic idealism, uncommon for poems of that period of devastating warfare. His succinct but poignant writing style still stands as a beautiful expression of poetry even today.

A Soldier
If I should die, think only this of me: That there's some corner of a foreign field that is forever England.
Rupert Brooke

Lord Byron - George Gordon, (1788-1824) The Sixth Baron Byron of Rochdale, Lord Byron was a British poet recognized for his rebellious and dark themes. He created the "Byronic hero," reflecting his thoughts of isolation and loneliness in his characters. He was one of the most acclaimed poets of the romantic movement and wrote "Don Juan," in 1824, an epic satire. Byron was notorious for his inclandestine love affairs and sometimes extreme lifestyle. He died trying to help Greece's independence from the Turks.

Agnostics
There is something Pagan in me that I cannot shake off. In short, I deny nothing, but doubt everything.
Lord Byron

Ann-Margret – actress, entertainer

Chapter Three

FAMOUS PERSONALITIES

Some may readily argue that all redheads are "personalities," and are at least famous among their friends and families, but these particular redheads have become well-known all across the world.

TELEVISION STARS

Lucille Ball - Born in 1911, Lucille Ball was first known early in her career as "Technicolor Tess", even though her hair wasn't naturally red. Enduring a B-movie star status during the 1940's, Lucille, with her husband Desi Arnez, finally became world-famous in the 1950's for her TV series with their show "I Love Lucy." She later divorced Desi and starred again with Vivian Vance in her next series, "The Lucy Show." Her films include *Stage Door* (1937) and *Mame* (1974). She later married Gary Morton, and passed away in 1988 after finishing her third comedy series.

Carol Burnett - Raised in family life that was traumatic at times (both her parents were alcoholics), as a child Carol Burnett escaped her unhappiness by performing little skits she created. She was a hit in several Broadway shows, and soon starred in her own television series after becoming popular when she dyed her hair bright red for the movie "Once Upon a

Mattress." Her TV show became one of the top comedy series, in league with Lucille Ball and Mary Tyler Moore, and featured such whacky talent as Tim Conway, Harvey Korman, Vicki Lawrence, and Dick Van Dyke.

After Burnett closed her award-winning series in 1978 ("We had our turn, and I wanted to leave before we ran out of ideas completely"), she went on to play dramatic parts in movies, receiving critical praise in the TV movie, "Friendly Fire", about an American mother whose enlisted son is accidently killed by his own troops during the Vietnam War.

Danny Bonaduce - Star of the 1970's television series "The Partridge Family," Danny was the redhaired son who was always spouting sarcastic observations of life around him. As an adult in real life, he had a series of legal problems which had him headed down the road to trouble. He pulled himself away from disaster and became a successful radio disc jockey. He credits the turnaround in his success to his wife, Gretchen. He is now a popular radio talkshow host in Chicago, and had a short-lived stint with his own TV talk show called "Danny!".

Cassandra Peterson - Born in a small town, Peterson used to dress up in costumes in her mother's shop to escape into the make-believe world of showbiz. Badly burned on her back and shoulders in a freak accident with a boiling kettle of water, she was taunted by the neighborhood children expressing their dislike of her scars. Cassandra dreamed of becoming a Las Vegas showgirl, and when she finally did, she thought she would be contented and satisfied after reaching that goal.

Then she met and dated Elvis Presley, who directed her to get into music, and she pursued her career as a rock singer for a few years before being discovered in Hollywood, but not for singing. After a few auditions, she was selected as "Elvira," the new hostess for a weekly presentation of corny and classic scary movies.

Dubbed the "Queen of Scream", Cassandra is well-known for her campy appearances during Halloween which she has turned into a lucrative business endorsing products and promoting her "Elvira" character.

Donny Most - Getting his first break as a teenager by landing a TV commercial, Donny then went on to become one of the most recognized characters on television for his role as "Ralph Malph" on the sit-com series "Happy Days." Leaving the series in 1980 for other projects, he returned for guest appearances, but was disillusioned with the scripts, feeling that more dignity was owed his redhaired character. He now works as a producer of specials, and has made few appearances publicly.

Conan O'Brien - A comedy writer who first got his start on the long-running television show, "Saturday Night Live," O'Brien was given the empty spot on late night television that was created when David Letterman left NBC for CBS in 1994. The puckish redhead now hosts his own late night television show, "Late Night With Conan O'Brien," a nationally syndicated talk show.

David Caruso – A stone face and bright redhair mark this male actor that took television by storm in 1993 in the controversial series "NYPD Blue." He left the show after the first season to pursue a career in the movies and *TV Guide* magazine voted him "Sexiest Man of the Month" in 1994. In 1995, he starred in the action movies "Kiss of Death" (with Nicholas Cage), and "Jade". He also starred in "Thief of Hearts," "China Girl," "Twins," and "An Officer and a Gentleman."

Marion Ross - A two-time Emmy nominee for her work as "Mrs. C" in the popular "Happy Days" television series, Marion Ross is one of the most-recognized "matriarchs" on television today. She is a versatile actress who has also starred in hundreds of episodes in other hit series such as "Brooklyn Bridge," "McGyver," "Glitter," and "Night Court," to name a few. She was raised in Minnesota as a teenager but attended San Diego State, where she won the "Most Outstanding Actress Award" as a drama student.

Jacklyn Zeman - Born in New Jersey, Miss Zeman grew up practicing the arts, taking ballet lessons at the age of five and eventually winning a scholarship in dance to the University of New York. A voluptuous and attractive redhead, Jacklyn worked with the Playboy Record Company and then made her big move to daytime soap operas with a debut on ABC's "One Life to Live." She then became popular as the character Bobbie Spencer on "General Hospital" in 1977. Her movies include "Young Doctors in Love," and "National Lampoon's Class Reunion."

About redhair, Jacklyn said: "When I became a teenager, I started experimenting with hair tints. In my twenties, I liked my redhead better than my experiments. Now I wouldn't dream of changing it until it turns grey!"

Shawntel Smith - Being the first redhaired Miss America in more than 50 years (see "Venus Ramey") has given Shawntel's year of service an adventurous aspect. "I remember when I competed in the (1995) Miss America Pageant, all my friends from Oklahoma held up this huge banner at the Boardwalk Parade that said 'RED RULES!'"

In grade school she was called "Red" and "Carrot Top", but the good-natured teasing helped bring about her positive self-image. "My hair made me feel a sense of individuality, and it attracted attention. My mother used to tell me that freckles were kisses from angels."

Scott Thompson, aka **"Carrot Top"** - Clownish standup comedian who uses silly sight gags for his jokes. Some fellow comedians find "Carrot Top" more of a clown than a standup comedian. Some redheads dislike his choice for a stage name.

Eric Stoltz – actor ("Memphis Belle," "Pulp Fiction," "Rob Roy," "The Prophecy," "Some Kind of Wonderful")

MOVIE STARS

Eric Stoltz - Born in 1962, this redhaired actor has starred in such dramatically acclaimed movies as "Mask" and "Some Kind of Wonderful". He is noted for being the consummate professional with his acting craft. A handsome man, Stoltz is a singularly intense individual and carefully chooses films for what he feels are their artistic merit. He once turned down a role in a movie because of a nude scene he thought was tasteless. In 1994, he starred and produced, "Bodies, Rest and Motion," which also featured Phoebe Cates and Bridgette Fonda. His star began to grow in 1995 and he appeared in two box office hits, "Rob Roy," and "Pulp Fiction," and in other films, the re-make of "Little Women," which starred Winona Ryder, and "The Prophecy," with Christopher Walken.

Arlene Dahl - A popular 50's movie actress, Miss Dahl once remarked, "I usually don't admit this, but I am supposed to be a direct descendent of Eric the Red." Although a beautiful redhead, she never really found a good run of movies to launch her career. She had starring roles in "Reign of Terror," "My Wild Irish Rose," "Bengal Bride," and "Journey to the Center of the Earth."

Sarah Bernhardt - (1844-1923) A famous French actress, Sarah Bernhardt was well-loved by people of many countries for her singing, acting, and sparkling personality. She was a beautiful woman in her day who always demanded the best of herself and those around her. Accompanied by a dry wit, she rarely was left with egg on her face. Before one performance in Chicago, an episcopalian bishop denounced Ms. Bernhardt as the "whore of Babylon" as did other clergyman of the period who disapproved of her passionate scenes in her plays. But such lambasting only acted as publicity for her stage performances, and after she was well-received in Chicago, she sent the bishop a check with a letter, which said:

"Your Excellency, I am accustomed, when I bring an attraction to your town, to spend $400 on advertising. As you have done half the advertising for me, I herewith enclose $200 for your parish."

Spencer Tracy - (1900-1967) A film actor famous for his movies with Katherine Hepburn and his great acting ability, Spencer Tracy starred in classics like "Boys Town," "Father of the Bride," and "Guess Who's Coming to Dinner." When a young actor asked Tracy for his expert advice on acting, the star simply replied, "Just learn your lines and don't bump into the furniture." His off-screen romance with Miss Hepburn was the topic of many gossip columnists, and although they admitted to being close friends, they never married or allowed the public to know how far and deep their relationship went.

Ann-Margret - One of the world's most glamorous and versatile superstars, Ann-Margret has been twice nominated for an Academy Award, won five

Golden Globe Awards and received four Emmy nominations for her television work. She draws sell-out crowds in Las Vegas, Atlantic City and Radio City Music Hall. Her popularity has made her a three-time winner of the "Female Star of the Year" award given by the United Motion Pictures Association.

Ann-Margret was discovered by legendary comedian George Burns and starred in her first movie along side of Bette Davis as her daughter in "A Pocketful of Miracles." After much cost by director George Sidney, he added an extra scene to the movie "Bye Bye Birdie," her first starring role, in which she sang an new song. The opening number catapulted her to fame. She has made 43 films to date, including hits such as "Cincinnati Kid," "Tommy," "Carnal Knowledge," "Stagecoach," and recently the popular movie "Grumpy Old Men," and its sequel, "Grumpier Old Men," with Jack Lemmon and Walter Matthau. She has also published a New York Times best-selling autobiography, "My Story."

Ann-Margret is truly one of the most beloved stars in the entertainment industry and is recognized as being very accommodating to her fans. She lives with her husband, Roger Smith, in Beverly Hills, California.

Lee Grant - Born Lyova Haskell Rosenthal, this famous actress once quipped, "if a guy comes up to me and says 'I know you,' the first thing I think is - were he and I lovers once?" She won a *Best Supporting Actress* Oscar for "Shampoo", and also starred in the melodramatic 1960's television series, "Peyton Place".

Ron Howard - Best known as "Opie" on the "Andy Griffith Show," little Ronny grew up surrounded by the showbiz life style. He went on to star in the smash hit movie "American Graffiti" and then the spin-off TV series "Happy Days". His real-life youth matched his screen-life as the good All-American boy, participating in school activities and being on his high school yell squad. Howard is now one of the most respected film directors in Hollywood, with huge movie successes including, "Splash," "Nightshift," "Cocoon," "Parenthood" (with Steve Martin) and "Backdraft."

Glenda Jackson - One of the few women to ever win two Oscars, Miss Jackson also played the part of a historical figure with redhair, Queen Elizabeth I, in a six-part BBC television series to which she received great critical acclaim. She also starred opposite Walter Matthau in "House Calls" and "Hopscotch".

Shirley MacLaine - Actually born Shirley Beaty, Miss MacLaine has been a prolific actress who has been nominated six times for Academy awards, and won an Oscar for her acting in "Terms of Endearment" with Jack Nicholson. She also produced an Oscar-nominated documentary on China called "You Can Get There From Here", and starred in several Emmy-winning TV specials. The sister of actor Warren Beatty, she has been involved in what some people termed "oddball philosophies" dealing with reincarnation and "New Age" philosophies, none of which hurt her career or popularity. She is the only woman accepted as a member of the "Rat Pack," a social "club" once consisting of mega-stars Frank Sinatra, Sammy Davis, Jr., Dean Martin, Joey Bishop and Peter Lawford. She is definitely agreed by many in the entertainment industry to be a gifted actress and performer.

Bette Midler - A popular singer who declared herself "the last of the tacky ladies", the "Divine Miss M" was discovered by a young Barry Manilow, who produced her first album. She went on to star in "The Rose" in which she won critical acclaim for her acting. Once known for her chain smoking, hard drinking, and love of the wild night life, Midler sports a refreshing self-deprecating wit. She combines her shows with glitter and humor that has proved her to be an extremely popular performer. She has also been well-received for her starring roles in the movies "Down and Out in Beverly Hills," "Ruthless People," and "Outrageous Fortune."

Robert Redford - With his handsome face and great talent, Robert Redford has done much for the redhead image. He has starred in many great movies, "The Sting," "Butch Cassidy and the Sundance Kid," "Downhill Racer," "Three Days of the Condor," "The Way We Were," "All the President's Men," and "Brubaker" to name a few. But he didn't stop there and went on to direct "Ordinary People," which grabbed him an Oscar for "Best Picture" of 1980. He created some murmurs of protest on his racy "Indecent Proposal" in 1993, which he starred and directed.

He had a big movie hit in 1994 with the Academy Award nominated "Quiz Show," about chicanery in the television game show arena. He loves Utah, skiing, and is an outspoken supporter of the environment.

Janet Gaynor - (1906-1984) She was the first person to win an Academy Award in 1928 for her acting in three films, "Seventh Heaven," "Sunrise," and "Street Angel." She easily made the transition from silent films to "talkies," a feat that couldn't be done by many of the silent film era actors.

One of her best movies was "A Star is Born" with Fredric March. Born Laura Gainer, she had wowed audiences with her redhaired beauty and her romantic characters she played, usually as a "waif" that people would sympathize with in her scenes. She once said, "I would have made a lousy siren, but then Garbo would not have been a good waif." Franklin Roosevelt described her as being "cute as a button."

Miss Gaynor was critically injured in a car accident with a drunk driver in 1982, and died from continuing complications two years later. Actor James Stewart remarked, "...she was well-liked by all who knew her. She had a wonderful career and as long as movies last, she will never be forgotten."

Willie Nelson - (1933-) A popular country singer, Willie Nelson is best known for his straggled red-grey hair, close-cut beard, and a bandana tied around his head. His voice is rough and down-to-the-ground, but his sorrowful and poignant style is endearing to his fans, making him one of the most popular country singers of all time. A movie was made in which he starred, "The Redheaded Stranger," named after a song that he wrote. (See "The Redheaded Stranger")

Maureen O'Hara - Probably the most beautiful redhaired actress to ever grace the silver screen, Miss O'Hara has typified the fiery spirit that best describes redheads. In 1955, at the height of her career, she told an interviewer her beliefs on being redhaired:

"It's nice having redhair. Men have a more permanent thought about a redhaired girl than they do about a blonde. Men think of blondes generally more as a brief flash. A redhead is equally exciting to a man, but he gives her more than a fleeting thought. (Holds out her arm) Freckles...all over! I've never had a suntan in my life!"

On colors – "Green is usually a bad color for redheads because it sometimes reflects in the shadows on their faces, especially under the eyes... I hold anything green up to my face and look at myself hard before I buy it. Very pale pink is wonderful for redheads. Not candystick pink."

Her last movie was with John Wayne in "Big Jake." Her past popular movies include "How Green Was My Valley," "The Quiet Man," "Sentimental Journey," "Miracle on 34th Street," and "The Spanish Main," among many others.

Danny Kaye - (1913-1987) An American actor, Danny Kaye was well-known around the world for his silly gestures and verbal patter. Born David Daniel Kominski, he joined a dance team after presenting a comic routine at resorts in the Catskill Mountains. After migrating to Hollywood, he was discovered for his high-paced clown antics and went on to make several popular films, including "The Inspector General," "The Wonder Man," and "The Secret Life of Walter Mitty." He credited most of his success to the material prepared by his wife and coach, Sylvia Fine.

Dame Ellen Terry - (1847-1928) A British actress well-known for her Shakespearean roles, Miss Terry was a friend and foil for George Bernard Shaw, another famous redhead. When she was in her early fifties, though still popular, she complained that nobody would write a play for her now that she was a grandmother. When Shaw heard about what she said, he immediately wrote "Captain Brassbound's Conversion" exclusively for her. She received great acclaim for her role as Lady Cicely Waynfiete in the play, but said of her friend mischievously, "He only did it out of a natural desire to contradict." Shaw always wrote romantic letters to her, but she was smart enough to never meet him on anything other than a professional friendship. They remained friends throughout their lives. In her biography, "The Story of My Life," she wrote – *"Imagination, industry, and intelligence -"the three I's"- are all indispensable to the actress, but of these three the greatest is, without doubt, imagination."*

Clara Bow - (1905-1965) Proclaimed the "It Girl" and the spirit of the 1920's Jazz Age ("Roaring

Twenties"), Clara Bow was the first redhaired motion picture star. A definite epitomy of the "vivacious redhead" stereotype, she was sexy, provocative, scandalous, and daring, but with an apparent sense of humor. After winning a beauty contest, Miss Bow went to Hollywood and landed a part in "Down to the Sea in Ships" (1925). She then gained her most fame by starring in the movie, "It," and "Mantrap," but was disregarded by most critics. Even though she was extremely popular, her various scandals and her inability to make the transition to sound movies forced her to retire. She married western film star Rex Bell and remained in Hollywood until her death.

Arthur Godfrey - (1903-1984) Well-known radio and television announcer, Godfrey was sometimes referred to as "The Redhead." He starred in several movies, including "The Glass Bottom Boat," and "Where Angels Go, Trouble Follows."

Scott Grimes - (1972-) Young actor best-known for his part as the son in a family being attacked by alien criminals in the movie, "Critters," Scott is also a talented musician. A television series regular on "Party of Five," (Fox Television), Scott first was told to put a brown rinse in his hair, but they finally agreed to let him keep it red. He also starred in the movie hit "Crimson Tide," and guest starred on many television series. He has a band called, "Scott Grimes and the Misdemeanors," with an A&M record produced by Herb Albert.

Susan Morrow - According to "Who's Who in Hollywood," by David Ragan, Miss Morrow is "one of the loveliest redheads ever on screen." She didn't remain on screen very long, though. Her 1960's movies include "Macabre," "Gasoline Alley," "Battle Cry," and the forgettable "Cat Women on the Moon."

Elsa Lanchester - (1902-1986) Miss Lanchester was a talented film and stage actress, whose roles encompassed such movies as the "Bride of Frankenstein," and "Come to the Stable," the latter which she was nominated for an Oscar. Having a witty and self-deprecating sense of humor, she became the darling of the serious drama crowd, and later married talented actor Charles Laughton.

She was a prolific stage actress, having appeared in more than 3,000 appearances in the 1940's and 50's, and her dance prowess and dramatic readings fascinated and delighted the upper-crust of the arts society, including her good friends redhaired Evelyn Waugh and Osbert Sitwell, and Aldous Huxley. Other movies she starred in were "Mary Poppins," "Lassie Come Home," "That Darn Cat," and her last movie was "Murder by Death."

Woody Allen - Born Allen Stewart Konisberg, Woody grew up in Brooklyn's Flatbush section, where he says he told the other kids his name was Frank, but "they still beat me up." Writing some one-liners for TV personalities, he became well-known as a stand-up comic and playwright. He is best appreciated for his dry, angst-ridden wit, which surfaces in his movies like, "Sleeper", "Play it Again Sam", and "Annie Hall".

Allen won Academy awards for his movie, "Hannah and her Sisters" and is recognized as one of the foremost movie directors today.

Susan   Hayward - Born in 1917 as Edythe Marrenner, beautiful Susan Hayward would struggle through her early years in the shadow of her talented older sister, Florence. Most in her family were flaming redheads, and in the book, "Red," (by Robert LaGuardia) about Hayward's life, an excerpt states: *"...when she began in the first grade of Public School 181, the boys insulted her by calling her 'Red' and 'Pepper Pot' and 'Carrot top' and 'Bricktop.' One day, as she was walking home from school, a boy teased her with one of the names. She answered back and he socked her. Schoolbooks in hand, she sat down on the front steps of her building with tears in her eyes.*

Her father, heading out the door on his way to work, sat down beside her and she told him what happened. He looked at his youngest daughter and said, "Always hit back... remember this: the harder they hit you, the higher you'll bounce, if you are a good ball to start with. If not, you might as well give up anyway." From that point on, she learned to become a fighter, in all stages of her life."

Miss Hayward would go on to a meteoric but scandal-ridden career in the movies, and troubled by her inability to accept love, she finally died of a debilitating disease. Her best movies, "I'll Cry Tomorrow," "With a Song in My Heart," and "I Want to Live" which brought her much acclaim, were almost a mirror of her tragic life.

James Cagney (1899-1986) An American actor noted for his portrayals of tough characters in films, James Cagney actually got his first shot in show business as a "chorus girl" in 1919. His star was soon catapulted to the top in *Public Enemy* (1931), and he became one of the most-watched male actors in the 30's and 40's. Cagney was also a wonderful dancer, but had only a few roles in which to show his talents. He did a musical, though, and won an Academy Award in 1942 for *Yankee Doodle Dandy* in which he sang a few songs. Cagney had a direct approach to acting, once saying "Never settle back on your heels. Never relax, if you relax, the audience relaxes. And always mean everything you say."

Sterling Holloway - Perfectly cast in movies as a country bumpkin, Holloway mugged with his goofy face and whiny, high-rasped voice that became his trademark. Playing the role of "Waldo" in the '50's TV series, "Life of Riley," he established himself as a recognizable character by his unusual vocal style, which made him a sought-after voice for many Wait Disney cartoons. He also starred in over 100 films, including "Casey at Bat," with Wallace Beery.

Red Buttons - Born Aaron Chwatt, Red got his stage name after taking a job as a bellboy at Dinty Moore's Tavern in the Bronx. With his redhair and a uniform with 48 buttons on it, his customers tagged the teenaged Chwatt with his present name. As a dry-witted comedian, he landed a half-hour series on television in the '50's, and even though it only lasted two seasons, it did well-enough for him to continue a successful nightclub and stage act. He also did a few films, including "The Longest Day," and "The Poseidon Adventure."

Darren McGavin - A strong-featured "Irish -looking" actor who starred in hundreds of character roles for films since the 1940's, some of Darren McGavin's memorable performances were in "The Man with the Golden Gun," and "No Deposit, No Return."

Deborah Kerr - Born in Switzerland, Miss Kerr had a prolific career, but her acting persona is widely recognized as being the perfect governess, a role she played in many films. Softly pretty, she played parts that highlighted her proper manners, stiff determination, and feminine grace. She has an excellent track record for appearing in quality movies, starring in lead roles for "From Here to Eternity," "The King and I," "Heaven Knows, Mr. Allison," "The Sundowners," "Prisoner of Zenda," "The Night of the Iguana," "King Solomon's Mines" and more. (See "Movie Dialogue")

Marcia Mae Jones - Born in 1924, Marcia was a child actress of the '30's who was popular for her bratty and spiteful roles, probably because (according to "Who's Who in Hollywood") of her "round freckled face and curly red hair." She starred in movies during her childhood that included "The Champ," "King of

Jazz," "Adventures of Tom Sawyer," "Anne of Windy Poplars," and "The Little Princess." In her later years, she played character roles on many television series, such as "Streets of San Francisco," and "Barnaby Jones."

Van Johnson - Born in 1916, Van Johnson was a favorite actor of the 1940's, and has continued a casual, but successful acting career up into the present. He is best known for his roles as the "other guy," and has starred in the films "The Caine Mutiny," "Thirty Seconds over Tokyo," and "Wives and Lovers," to name a few.

Jack Warden - Best-known for his role as the suicidal judge in "Justice for All," with Al Pacino, Jack Warden is one of the most respected character actors in the business. You might remember him as the beer-drinking coach of "The Bad News Bears Break Training," or the crazily competitive used-car sales-man always trying to ruin co-actor Kurt Russell in "Used Cars." He also starred in his own television series in the 1980's called "Crazy Like A Fox".

Michael Kopelow - As the long-haired redhead "dude" in the 1994 movie "The Stoned Age," Michael Kopelow represented the misguided but sensitive redhead party guy in the early 1970's. Other movies he appeared in are "Don't Tell Mom The Babysitter's Dead," with Christine Applegate, and "Point Break," with Patrick Swayze. He also is a musician and singer.

Chapter Four

SPORTS HEROES

Jack Nicklaus - (1940-) A world-champion professional golfer, Jack has won several major tournaments, including being a five-time winner of the Masters Golf Tournament. Nicklaus had beaten Arnold Palmer at the 1962 US Open, and Palmer remarked, "Now that the big bear's out of the cage, everybody better run for cover." Slightly overweight in his younger years, Nicklaus answer was: "I'm hungry as a bear, but I'm gonna slim down and go for the gold." He became known as the "Golden Bear."

Red Auerbach - (1917-) Born Arnold Jacob Auerbach, "Red" is considered to be the all-time premiere basketball coach. As a respected author, sports commentator, and lecturer, he is an image of the redhead fighting spirit.

According to longtime Red Auerbach watcher, Bill Livingston of the Cleveland Plain Dealer, it seemed to him that *Sports Illustrated* magazine painted a portrait of Red at the time he was the Boston Celtics' general manager that made him sound like the "nation's doting uncle."

"I've seen his act," protests Livingston. "Red Auerbach is a bullying, conniving old maestro of the double-deal and the broken rule. He's a leftover from the dance hall and dingy gym era of the NBA. The game has moved uptown since Red's early days, but

Auerbach's ethics can still be as dark as a blind alley, as crabbed and cramped as the upper berth on the night train to Fort Wayne. I mean, really, would you want to be like a 65-year-old man who runs onto the court during a players' brawl and shouts at Moses Malone, 'Hit me, you big SOB.' I've always regretted that Malone didn't make Auerbach the first redhead on the moon by taking him up on that one."

But Mr. Auerbach doesn't pay attention to such opinions. He does state that, "It's easier to go around with the nickname "Red" than "Arnold.""

Red Grange - (1903-91) An outstanding American football player from Forksville, Pennsylvania, Grange was an All-American halfback (1923-25) at the University of Illinois, scoring 31 touchdowns and gaining 3,367 yards. In his professional career with the Chicago Bears (1925-35) he scored 1,058 points. A modest guy, he once replied when asked to explain his great ability to elude tacklers: "No one ever taught me, and I can't teach anyone. If you can't explain it, how can you take credit for it?" After he retired from football, he became a radio and television sportscaster.

Bill Walton - (1952 -) A graduate and star of UCLA, Walton went on to acclaim as a potent center for such teams as the Portland Trailblazers, the Los Angeles Clippers and the Boston Celtics. He has won several honors for his basketball prowess, including the Sullivan Memorial Award.

Dave Stapleton - Playing for the Red Sox, Stapleton doesn't remember too much negativity about his redhair, except being called "Woody Woodpecker." A steady ballplayer, he figured prominently in many winning seasons for the Red Sox.

Boris Becker - In 1985, at seventeen years of age, Boris Becker became the youngest Wimbleton Tennis champion. He is one of the most-feared tennis players, known for his blistering power serve that has left many of his opponents tripping over themselves. A native of Germany, Boris is one of the hottest draws in tennis. Some say that he may become the greatest tennis player of all time. During a television interview with Johnny Carson in early 1987, when asked what he looks for in a girl, he replied, "You know, I'm a man... you're a man.. we like women." Since 1989, he has won the British and U.S. Open singles titles repeatedly.

Alexi Lalas - The first United States-born soccer player selected to play in Italy's first division, which is considered the world's best soccer league in the professional arena. With much publicity coming off of the 1994 World Cup games, Lalas, a goateed and long-haired redhead, was thrown into the international spotlight for his exceptional playing on the U.S. Soccer Team.

Danny Chandler - World Champion motorcross racer who was considered the best in the world from

1979 until 1985 when he was paralyzed from an accident. His spirit drove him, even though he is a quadriplegic, to become a major promoter of mountain bike racing and motorcrosses. He even designed a ski-wheelchair so that he could race other wheelchair-bound athletes in the snow. After crashing in his wheelchair while doing some stunt, Chandler said that some guys told him that he was crazy. Chandler relished their sentiments and said "I think that's cool."

A streak of fire, a breath of flame,
eluding all who reach and clutch,
A gray ghost thrown into the game
that rival hands may never touch,
A rubber bounding, blasting soul,
whose destination is the goal –
Red Grange of Illinois

Grantland Rice, American Sportswriter

Quick List of Redhaired Sports Stars

Leon Ames - Baseball
Earl Blaik - Football coach
Christian Cagle - Football
Don Budge - Tennis
Donna Caponi - Golf
Harold Carlson - Football coach
JoAnne Carner - Golf
Freddie Cochran - Boxer
John Davis - Baseball, Football
Lowell Dawson - Football
Mary Dwyer - Golf
Thomas Hearden - Football
Ralph Kress - Baseball
Rod Laver - Tennis champion
John Murray - Baseball
Archie Manning - NFL Quarterback
Thomas Owens - Baseball
Irving Pearlman - Football
Sidney Quarrior - Football
Charles Ruffing - Baseball
Henry Sanders - Football Coach
Bernard Sarachek - Basketball
Chris Schlacter - Football
Vicki Singleton - Golf
James C. Smith - Baseball
Cody Snyder - champion rodeo rider
Gary Bettman - NHL Commissioner
Dan (Rusty) Staub - Baseball
Norman Strader - Football
Eric Tipton - Football
George Wolfe - Basketball

Danny Bonaduce – actor, talk show host ("Partridge Family" television series)

Chapter Five

STRANGE TALES

The Queen Who Saw Red

Redhaired Venus Ramey was the 1944 Miss America queen who inspired the long-lasting but little-known rumor that redheads were never allowed to win another Miss America pageant. It seems that Venus won the title when the pageant was held in September, and it forced her to a three-and-a-half month tour schedule which exhausted her so much that she couldn't take advantage of the opportunities the talent scouts offered when they had seen her perform during the pageant.

She tried to convince the pageant officials to skip the remaining part of 1944 so that she could represent the following year 1945 and subsequently bring the queen's reign to a full year. They didn't listen and gave, according to her, a "cheap" and "mishandled" publicity tour as queen. She claimed it ruined her timing for her chances at a singing career. Out of spite, she still went ahead and toured nightclubs singing a biting satire of a song called "I'm a Miss America - So What?"

She was nicknamed "Lust Bust" for her voluptuous bosom, a record measurement still unbeaten in the Miss America Pageants. Asked what her opinions were on the present pageant judging focus, she stated, "This new emphasis on brains is a lot of hooey. If they really wanted to have a brain thrust, they should put them in a hall and let them fill out forms for two hours to see who comes up with the most multiple-choice answers."

After her stint as a singer, she finally returned home to Kentucky, married and had two children. As far as another redhead winning the Miss America title, Shawntel Smith won over fifty years later in 1995. (See "Shawntel Smith")

Hep Us Now

On a British television program that aired in 1960, a story was told about a captain of a merchant vessel who overheard some of his crew muttering angrily. When he asked them what was bothering them, the crew told him they were worried that there was a redhaired woman aboard, along with their cargo of iron ore, and they thought it was a bad omen. The captain ordered them back to work and the ship arrived safely at its destination.

Redhot Revolvers

Redheads or redbearded men are quicker on the draw than most other cowboys of the Old West according to Professor Hans von Hentig, who studies criminology. Jesse James, Sam Brown, and Wild Bill Hickock were supposed redheads, according to von Hentig. Some of the earlier scientists and sociologists thought that redhead men were more violent or became criminals easier because of the teasing in their youth, which allegedly created an inferiority complex leading to anti-social behavior.

Call The Humane Society

In ancient Rome, to avert the red mildew and excessive heat from the sun upon their fields, the farmers used to kill redhaired puppies and pour the blood over the soil in tribute to the god Robigus.

Cast a Red Spell

Red-haired people are said to possess an aura of magnetism and mystic power in a free-floating form and are capable of projection more than other people. Even long ago in the days of ancient Egypt, redheads were feared as the most potent of witches and sorcerers. Set, the sorcerer brother of Osiris, was said to have been a redhead. [See Folklore]

Redfoot

In Wuhan, China, there have been numerous confirmed sightings of a 7-foot hairy creature that has been roaming the Shennongjia Forest, with over 300 reports of the "Ye Ren" or "wild man" being recorded since 1920. The creature has been compared to the "Sasquatch/Bigfoot" and "Abominable Snowman" monsters, but Ye Ren is even more plausible, according to Li Jian, a historian who began studying the Ye Ren since 1981.

One thousand footsteps, each measuring 18 inches long were discovered covering a distance of almost a mile. Most of the witnesses who have spotted the wild man have said that he has long, thick, matted red hair. Samples of the hair have been found and analyzed, and were dissimilar to human, ape, or pigs hair. There have been stories about the wild men dating back to 3,000 years ago, when one was captured and given to a king of the Eastern Chou Dynasty as a gift.

Redtown?

It is reported that some towns in Europe have almost a predominately redhaired populace. Some of the more redhaired areas include Salisbury, England, (which is the home of the legendary Knights of the Round Table), and also Lausanne, Switzerland.

United in Red

There have been several clubs formed to organize redheads throughout history, some documented as far back as 500 A.D. if you count the gangs of Scottish redheads. More towards the present, there have been several. The largest is **Redheads International,** with a membership of over 25,000 as of 1995. Members want redheads to be seen as the exciting and wonderful people that they are, with pride and poise in the face of a sometimes colorless world. Non-redheads who love redheads are also welcome to join. They offer redhead promotional items ("Don't Mess With Red" bumperstickers) and a quarterly newsletter called the

Redheader, which features interviews with redhaired celebrities and other redhead events and facts.

Redheads International
537 Newport Center Drive #119
Newport Beach, CA 92625

Another chapter of Redheads International is:

The Redheads of Tucson, headed up by Joanne Diggins, mother of four, two of which are redheads. She holds picnics and puts a redhead float in the St. Patrick's Day parade. Wendy's Hamburgers of Tucson sponsors their event. (The Wendy's symbol is a little redhaired girl). If you are in the Tucson area and you want to join, write to PO Box 26906, Tucson, AZ 85726.

Redhead Piano Bar - Founded in 1993 by Eileen Wolcoff, the Redhead Piano Bar is an upscale nightclub establishment located in Chicago, Illinois. Ms. Wolcoff named the bar in honor of her appreciation of her own redhair. She started the business because she was interested in rekindling the piano bar scene where people could go someplace classy but low-key. Designed with an old film noir motif, the bar is located in a Brownstone building and the interior features photos of movie stars and sheet music from the 20's. She promises that redheads and their guests will receive the "red carpet treatment".

The Redhead Piano Bar is located at 16 West Ontario, in Chicago, Illinois.

Temper, Temper

Charged with murdering her father and step-mother in 1892, Lizzie Borden's case became one of the most famous in American criminal history. She was finally acquitted, but the public still viewed her as guilty. At the time of the murders, she was a 32-year old Sunday School teacher still living at home with her parents in Fall River, Massachusetts. She remained there, much to the consternation of the local residents, until her death.

The crime has been the subject of many books, stage plays, and even a musical revue, all presenting different conclusions of her guilt or innocence. Even a children's song became popular during her lifetime:

Lizzie Borden took an axe
and gave her mother forty whacks
When she had saw what she had done
She gave her father forty-one.

Can't Stop Red

When red-haired poetess Elizabeth Siddal committed suicide, her husband, Dante-Gabriel Rossetti, buried her with a bundle of her last poems. Later on, when he was in great need of money, he asked a friend of his to exhume the poems for publication. When the friend opened the lid, legend has it that he was flabbergasted at what he saw; Miss Siddal's redhair had continued to grow, almost filling the whole coffin. However, medical experts say that hair does not grow after death. The friend was probably not aware of how long Miss Siddal's hair was at the time of her death.

Big Reds

In Poland there is a myth of the "Dziwozony," or "Wild Women," who are big redheaded women with hairy bodies and cold hearts. The Dziwozony are said to be fond of little boys, and know much about the ways of nature. It was usually a story told by mothers to keep their young sons from wandering off into the woods, where the wild women supposedly roamed.

Another Marx was a Red, too

Harpo Marx, a member of the Marx Brothers comedy team, became famous by being a very animated mime in a blonde wig, but he also wore a red wig. He didn't use it often because it didn't show up very well in the black and white movies of the day.

Red of Troy

Helen of Troy, who was the daughter of Greek gods, Zeus and Leda, was considered the most beautiful woman in Greek mythology. Paris, the prince of Troy received Helen as a prize for choosing Aphrodite as the fairest of the goddesses. When Paris took Helen, it caused the start of the Trojan Wars.

Red Ghosts

In ancient Celtic beliefs, red was the color of the otherworld. In the story of "Da Derga's Hostel," the doomed king knows his end is near when he envisions three redhaired men riding three red horses and wearing red equipment.

The Book

The directory of nobility and royalty of the European courts during the Middle Ages was called "The Red Book," and was considered the official listing of Who's Who of that period in history.

Hide the Shovel

The ancient Egyptians paid homage to their god Osiris by burying redhaired men alive. (See also "Robigus")

Goldilocks

Ancient alchemists tried to turn base metals to gold by mixing as a main ingredient the powder from the "Philosopher's Stone," otherwise known as "red tincture." The purest gold was called "red."

Sometimes in medieval stories or descriptions, the word "golden-haired" was meant to describe light redhair. Blondes were called "flaxen-haired," black hair was "raven-haired," and brunettes were referred to as "amber-haired."

Hey City!

Ruse is a city in northeast Bulgaria on the Danube River south of Bucharest, Romania. Founded as a Roman fortress in the second century A.D., it later became a city named for the invading armies of Barbarossa when it became a principal stronghold for the Turks of the Ottoman Empire. Sometimes spelled "Russe" or "Rousse," it has been called several different names through history, including, "Roustchouk," which may have been Old Serbian for "Red City." Some historians also believe Ruse was named as a result of the influence of the Rus Dynasty of Russia during the 8th century.

Powerful Color

In certain cultures and periods in history, Monarchs, kings and other rulers were thought to have the best qualities if they had redhair, wore red, or carried their pageantry in mostly red. Heraldry was best done in red (as in a red carpet welcome) as it represented honor, fire and strength. Conversely, in the Victorian era, red was the color of shame, possibly because of its allusion to passion.

"Bring on the Redhead!" – from animatronic pirates on the Disneyland ride, "Pirates of the Caribbean."

Don't Mess With Red

In old Irish lore, young golden-haired girls were often stolen by fairies and goblins who were fascinated by the girls' beauty. In "The Golden Haired Girl of Urst," a popular Irish folk tale about a light redhaired young girl, the mother of the girl was bewitched by fairies before giving birth to her, and the girl was born with beautiful features and hair. Her hair was so wondrous that it had magical qualities and could not be cut or set in any fashion; it had to remain long and flowing in its hundreds of ringlets. Everyone would look in awe at this lovely creature, and she was the pride of the town.

An old witch heard about the girl's hair and beauty, snuck up on the poor child while she was asleep and cut off her beautiful curls. The girl, void of her locks, fell ill and died, and the fairies were enraged. They recast a spell on the girl, and before the townsfolk could close the lid on her coffin, her hair had grown to fill the box. The fairies then put a spell on the witch that caused her to wander endlessly among the fairies' domain, where they pestered her until she was whisked away forever.

No More Blondes

Blondes will soon be extinct, according to an article featured in the October, 1916, issue of *Literary Digest*. The article, titled "Chestnut Threads Among the Gold," declares that there is a growing controversy (with racist overtones) that blondes and golden tresses, and light brunettes, are being filtered out because of the influx of Russian and Latin immigrants. The article states that all Americans' hair will soon be a dull brown and "it is not the golden brown, either, nor anything you can be ecstatic about: it is a mud color."

By now, the writer is beseeching her readers: "Where are all the golden-haired girls? Airy, fairy Lillian, where is she?"

Then in a note of happy but tentative relief, the writer concedes to the strength of redhair: "Still, there is cheer; here and there the glorious redhaired girl still holds the fort, a brilliant spot of beauty in the wide monotony (of brownettes)."

Captain Red

In 1767, an Irishman by the name of Hugh O'Conor was appointed the governor of Texas by the Spanish viceroy. In those days, many Irish patriots went to other countries to fight against England, and were rewarded for their efforts. O'Conor rose rapidly through the ranks of officers in Spain and was made a knight in the esteemed order of Calatrava. As governor (and captain of the Los Adaes presidio) in Texas, O'Conor made a name for himself, and among the Indians of the area, he became known as "Capitan Colorado," or "Captain Red." His red beard and fair complexion made him stand out and today O'Conor's nickname is the name of one of the most beautiful states in America.

Chapter Six

FOLKLORE

Folklore is an interesting topic to research; there are so many variations to a theme with every story seeming to have a different angle on any particular subject. Some folklore seems contradictory to the beliefs of the day, showing that many times stories are created to support or enhance a particular opinion. Usually, folklore is just romanticized versions of people's thoughts on subjects that they don't understand or have an established scientific truth.

Red Rat

In the early Middle Ages, many people mistrusted redheads and even feared them. They believed that persons of the redhaired persuasion practiced deceit, a belief that probably came from the widespread notion that Judas Iscariot, the disciple who betrayed Jesus, was a redhead.

Too Hot too Handle?

It is said that the Brahmins of India (the upper segment of the Hindu caste system) were forbidden to marry redhaired women. According to the India Consulate in San Francisco, this may have been a law pertaining mostly to not marrying outside their religion, since they say there are no redhaired Indians.

Elopement Time

Irish farmers once did not want their daughters to marry redheads because many tinkers and vagrants had redhair. The theory behind this prejudice was that in Ireland, redheads were once persecuted, so they banded together with the gypsies and wandered the countryside doing menial jobs as "tinkers". These tinkers were among the first migrants to Scotland, hence they have the highest redhead ratio in the world; 14% of the Scottish population has redhair.

Good Guys

There are a few countries of the world whose people greatly admire and appreciate redheads. The country most likely to treat redheads with affection is Italy, well-known for its great paintings featuring redheads. Greece is also a country that is thought to favor redheads for their believed mythical qualities.

Name Your Poison

During earlier centuries, redheads in certain cultures were popularly believed to be unreliable, deceitful, and quick-tempered. The fat of a redhaired person was in demand as an ingredient for poison! An anonymous chapman (Old English for "dealer" or "merchant") said that "flattery, like the plague, strikes into the brain of man, and rageth in his entrails when he can, worse than the poison of a redhair'd man." [*Bussy d' Ambois*]

Stop Those Windmills

In Holland, redheads are still considered to be agents of misfortune, most likely because of the memories from the invasions of the Danes and Vikings, a commonly redhaired people.

The Red Planet

Peter Ouspensky was a Russian mystic and philosopher who once said that redheads were governed by energy from the planet Mars. A study by astrologist Judith Hill of San Francisco, California into redheads and their birth signs have not proved him wrong. (See "Martians - The Red Planet")

Red San

A mythical creature of Japan, Shojo is a personification of merriment and drinking. Believed to have arrived by magical ways, Shojo has long red hair that hangs down to the floor and he dresses in bright decorative robes of red and gold. Many believe that he created Saki, an alcoholic Japanese drink.

We Do Windows, Too

The heroes of the Melanesian culture, Gwau Meo and Sina Kwao, are sons of the Sun. They are said to slay monsters, perform great deeds and bring new culture (foods, magic, weapons, etc.) to the island of Mala in the Solomon Islands in the Pacific Ocean.

Chapter Seven

PROVERBS

The Maori tribesman of New Zealand have a proverb that says, *"Red hair, chief's hair,"* which indicated that the young man with the reddest hair would soon be chief.

*"A red beard and a black head
catch him with a good trick and take him dead."*
Old English Proverb

"Salute no redhaired man nearer than thirty feet off, and even so hold three stones in the fist wherewith to defend thyself."
Old English Proverb

"In Donegal, if a girl is born with redhair it is a sign that there was a pig under the bed."
Irish Proverb

"Never lodge at redhaired people's houses, for these be folks that are to drede."
Old English Proverb

"Do not let the shadow of a redheaded person fall upon you. It might give you bad luck."
Old English Proverb

"If you happen to walk any distance between two red-headed girls, it is a sign that you will soon be very rich."
Scottish Proverb

"Red-haired people cannot make good butter, for the butter always ends up with a slight tang to it."
Old English Proverb

"If a person has redhair on the top of his head or the back of his neck, then he will be wealthy."
Proverb of Madagascar

"It's unlucky to meet a redhead on the first morning of the month of May."
Old English Proverb

"Redheaded women are either violent or false, and usually are both."
French Proverb

"True fortune's promise is a redhaired madonness"
-Ibid.

"An honor it is to have a child with redhair."
Danish Proverb

"If you should pass a redhead in the street, spit and turn around."
Corsican Proverb

"If you pass by three redhaired people, you will win the state lottery."
Polish Proverb

Chapter Eight

REDHEADS SURVEY RESULTS

What Redheads Think About Their Image
In 1983, a survey was taken by Redheads International among 500 redheads from all over the U.S. to find out how they felt about being redhaired. There seems to be a general consensus that redheads sometimes do not get the respect they feel they deserve. The following questions were asked (*more than one answer allowed*):

"What do you hate being called the most?,
85% - "Carrot-top" "Red," "I'd rather be dead than red."
10% - "Bozo," "The redhead is dead," "Flamebrain."
5% - "You're cute - for a redhead," "Matchstick," "Freckle-faced strawberry," "Woody Woodpecker," "Red, red, wet the bed," "Torch," "Is it real?" "Pinky," "Your head's bleeding," "Rusty."

"Were you teased as a kid?"
32% - a lot
59% - a little
9% - hardly

"Who's your favorite female celebrity?"
40% - Lucille Ball
23% - Ann-Margret
18% - Carol Burnett
11% - Stefanie Powers
5% - Linda Kelsey, Victoria Principal

3% - divided between the following: Tina Louise, Marilu Henner, Maureen O'Hara, Rhonda Fleming, Susan Hayward, Rita Hayworth, Deborah Kerr

Favorite Male Redhead
This part of the 1983 survey went mostly unanswered, proof of the fact that there is a woefully small amount of redheaded men in the movies and on television. Hopefully that will change now with actors David Caruso and Eric Stoltz

"Who's your favorite male redhead celebrity?"
89% - un-answered
3% - Ron Howard
2% - Red Buttons
1% - Donny Most
1% - divided among the following: Eric Stoltz, Red Skelton, Howdy Doody, Robert Redford, Harold Greene, Woody Allen, Bill Walton.

Redhaired Statistics
Out of 500 women polled in a 1985 survey, the results of the test showed some remarkable statistics on redheads and their ancestries; eye color by region, and eye color by ancestry. The majority of those who answered were between the ages of 20-40 years old.

Ancestry of Redheads Polled in U.S.
Below are the results broken down to several categories, as each sample professed to have ancestry to more than one country. The total amount of redheads out of 500 surveyed having some Irish ancestry is 324.

From the response, the following represents the breakdown of particular ancestries, most respondents indicating that they were of two or more different nationalities:

65%	Irish
27%	English
31%	German
14%	Scottish
7%	Italian
7%	French
5%	Swedish

It is interesting to note that by region, redheads with Irish descent made up 48% of those polled in the southwest United States. Equally, 41% of all Italian redheads polled lived on the east coast, but the Italian redheads only represented 10% of the total ancestry of all polled from that region. The majority ancestry from the east coast with redhair were the Irish, with 41%. The highest concentration of those who were of French ancestry (27%) were located in the west. The regional breakdown for ancestry in America is defined as follows *(out of 500)*:

Total Irish disbursement of those polled (195)
    East - 28%
    South - 20%
    Midwest - 17%
    Southwest - 12%
    West - 21%

Total English disbursement (134):
      East - 24%
      South - 18%
      Midwest - 17%
      Southwest - 9%
      West - 29%
Total German disbursement (155):
      East - 23%
      South - 16%
      Midwest - 23%
      Southwest - 7%
      West - 28%

Total French disbursement (36):
      East - 6%
      South - 25%
      Midwest - 19%
      Southwest - 11%
      West - 27%

Total Scottish disbursement (70)
      East - 25%
      South - 18%
      Midwest - 14%
      Southwest - 14%
      West - 27%

Total Italian disbursement (34):
      East - 41%
      South - 5%
      Midwest - 8%
      Southwest - 8%
      West - 29%

Eye Color

In the southwest United States, 55% of those polled were blue-eyed. Blue eyes took the field with 45% of all those polled.

The percentage of the eye color in redheads is as follows:

Blue	45%
Green	24%
Brown	18%
Hazel	12%

The following are the majority results of eye color by ancestry:

Blue eyes (*221 out of 500*)	Irish (44%)
Brown eyes (*90 out of 500*)	German (43%)
Green eyes (*117 out of 500*)	Irish (32%)
Hazel eyes (*60 out of 500*)	Irish (45%)

The breakdown of all American redhead ancestries' predominant eye color:

Irish	Blue (50%)
English	Blue (52%
German	Blue (40%)
French	Brown (36%)
Scottish	Blue (41%)

Cosmetic Favorites - Skin allergies seem to be prevalent among redheads, adding to the belief that most redheads are prone to have skin problems, including sunburning easily.

"Are you allergic to certain cosmetics?"
   42%   - Yes
   57%   - No
   1%   - No Answer

Redhaired women have a definite pride about their looks, and an overwhelming amount of them are happy with their status.

"Do you feel special and noticed as a redhead?"
   91%   - Yes
   3%   - No
   4%   - Don't Care
   1%   - No Answer

Even though the redhead woman feels special, she still has slight reservations about the problems that accompany redhair: sunburn, teasing, and 30% of all redheads are bothered by having pale or sensitive skin that doesn't tan.

"Are you 100% glad that you have redhair?"
   80%   - Yes
   19%   - No
   1%   - No Answer

Colors are important to redheads in the clothing they wear. The following are the colors most liked by redheads polled (in order of preference):

1. Earthtones (browns)
2. Blue
3. Green
4. Pink, peach
5. White
6. Yellow, grey
7. Lavender (write in choice)
8. Red
9. Black, magentas

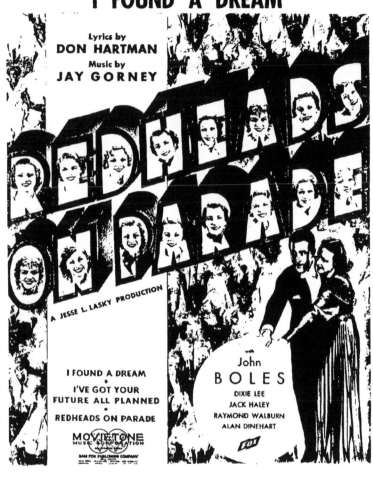

Chapter Nine

REDHEAD DIALOGUE AND TITLES

"Her hair is winter fire
            January embers
                        My heart burns there, too."
(from Stephen King's novel "It")

BOOKS

The Redhaired Lady - Written by Elizabeth Corbett in 1945, this sweeping novel was a character study of a beautiful redhaired lady named Cassandra. A married authoress, Cassandra was always writing books, but was unhappy in her marriage. She left her husband to explore New York nightlife in the 1920's, retaining a cynical view about men, but not for long, as she breezed through a whirlwind of affairs.
(Published by Doubleday)

Redhead in Red Square - written in 1969 by Debbie Sherwood, this story is an adventuresome tale about a former Hollywood starlet who puts on a red wig and travels to Russia for a summer of fun and gaiety.
(Published by Dodd)

The Redhaired Bitch - by Clifford Hanley is a novel written in 1969 about a millionaire who was willing to lose money on a play about Mary, Queen of Scots, so that his wife would have an acting vehicle to show her talents.

My Rotten Redheaded Older Brother - a children's story by Patricia Polacco about a young girl's travails with her redhaired older brother. Her opinion of his treatment of her is evident in the title of this book. *(Published by Simon and Schuster)*

The Redheaded Outfield - This short story by Zane Grey, first published in 1915, is about a baseball team with three redhead players in the outfield. The three characters; Red Gilbat, a "jack o'lantern, a will-o'-the-wisp, a weird, long-legged, long-armed redhaired illusive phantom," and Reddy Clammer, "... strutting, posing, talking, arguing, quarreling, - when he was not making a grandstand play," and Reddie Ray, "beautiful sight to see him run."

The story centers around a championship game and the personalities of these redheads. During the game when someone in the crowd yelled "redhead," Red Gilbat runs over and angrily asked "who called me redhead?" and from the crowd "all over the bleachers, from everywhere, came the obnoxious word." The "obnoxiously" described redheaded outfield went on to win the game.

Sherlock Holmes and the Redheaded League - In this story, a red-cressed pawnbroker, Jabez Wilson answered an advertisement that said the "Redheaded League" wanted to interview "redheaded men with sound body and mind." The job entailed copying the Encyclopedia Britannica for four pounds a week.

Wilson got the job. He was told that he would work four hours a day, and he could not leave under any circumstances. He worked at the job by himself for six weeks in a empty room, and he got paid promptly.

Suddenly, Wilson stopped getting paid and the office door was locked. Not being able to find his employer, he went to Holmes for help.

Wilson describes his awe when he first went to answer the ad: *"I never hope to see such a sight as that again, Mr. Holmes. From north, south, east, and west every man who had a shade of red in his hair had tramped into the city to answer the advertisement. Fleet Street was choked with redheaded folk, and Pope's Court looked like a coster's orange barrow."*

Redhead – A grade school children's book about a hot-tempered young redhaired girl who learns the value of friends and family to help her master self-control.
(By Jean Nielsen /Published by Funk & Wagnalls - 1961)

More...
Here are more books about redheads, most written in the late 1920's. These books may be hard to find:

"*Red*" - a South Sea romance by W.S. Maughum
"*Red*" - a biography of Susan Hayward, by Robert LaGuardia and Gene Arceri
"*Redheaded Brat*" - J.C. Hilder
"*Redheaded Country Girl*" - M.W. Jackson
"*Redheaded Woman*" - Katharine Brush (also a movie)
"*Redhair and Freckles*" - F.L. Pfalzgraf
"*Redbeard*" - H. Winslow

MOVIE DIALOGUE

King Solomon's Mines (1950) - The original screenplay and movie has Stewart Granger and redhaired Deborah Kerr out on the African plains in search of treasure. As guests of a local tribe, they view a dance and ritual where the tribesmen are singing, "Mensai - Benai - Kanubu". Miss Kerr asks Granger what they are shouting so fervently.

"They're chanting about the 'woman with the flaming hair'," Granger replied.

The Spanish Main (1945) - The movie, starring the beautiful Maureen O'Hara and dashing Paul Henreid, was about a 'good' pirate called "Barracuda" (Henreid) who attacked the ships of an evil Spanish governor. The beautiful young daughter (O'Hara) of a Viceroy is sent as a bride to the governor. Her ship was intercepted by the Barracuda, and he decided to keep the flame-haired beauty from being sold as a slave by his shipmates. He buys their "interests" in her for 50,000 "pieces-of-eight" gold coins, which his crew divides equally.

Later, in his quarters, Barracuda teases O'Hara about whether or not she was worth that much, because she was being obstinate. He jests about selling her on the slave market when they dock. He teasingly says that she may not be worth what he paid for her:

He: (eyeing her closely) *Maybe there are qualities that I overlooked...*
She: *You mean...such as my figure?*

122

He: *Quite possibly. It could bring in 5,000, maybe 4,000 pounds at the slave market...*
She: *...and my hair?*
He: *There is fire in it. That will bring in another 2,000 pounds!*

Thunderbolt and Lightfoot - a thriller starring Clint Eastwood and Jeff Bridges, who are looking for a hidden bag of cash while being chased by some thugs. In one scene, they meet two women and take them to a hotel. One of the women, a redhead, walks out on Bridges. Shrugging off his rejection, Bridges says to Eastwood, *"Redhaired women are bad luck anyways."* Actor George Kennedy played a bad guy named "Red" (he dyed his hair for the part).

"The thing about redheads is - lack of pigmentation." (James Belushi to Rob Lowe in the movie, "About Last Night")

Wraith - In this 1986 movie starring Charlie Sheen and Randy Quaid, a sleazy character named "Gutter-boy" uttered the infamous line, *"No longer will anyone beat me like a redheaded stepchild."* He wasn't a redhead. Unfortunately, he was killed later in the movie.

I.Q. - A motion picture comedy starring Tim Robbins, Meg Ryan and Walter Matthau (who plays Albert Einstein). One of Einstein's colleagues says to him, "We've got to get you a girl." Another scientist replies, *"Ya, a redhead!"*

Far Horizons - In a tale of Lewis and Clark's expedition in the early 1800's, Charlton Heston starred as a captain with Fred MacMurray as Meriwether Lewis and Donna Reed as their Shoshone Indian guide, Sacajawea. In one scene, Donna Reed tells Heston, *"I would like to see a woman with red hair,"* after asking what white women were like. In another scene, a Mandan Indian warrior tells another warrior that Reed *"belongs to the chief with the red hair."* He was referring to Charlton Heston, who had dyed his hair red for the part. Produced by Paramount.

Winchester 73 – In this action-packed movie starring James Stewart, a calvary soldier comments to another, *"My wife has brown hair with red in it. I hope my kid has brown hair with red in it."*

Unconquered – Tall, soft-talking Gary Cooper starred in this 1947 movie about Indian-fighting and gun-running during the 1700's. Paulette Godard is the redhead who is being sold as an indentured slave when Cooper comes to her rescue. As officers comment on the beauty of Godard and the aspect of purchasing her, one comments, "Yes, but I'm not taken to slavery." Another replies, *"That redhair could change a man's mind!"* Later, when Ms. Godard wants to escape, her captor tells her, *"There's no town in these colonies big enough to hide that redhair of yours."*

MOVIE TITLES

The Redheaded Stranger - Redhaired singer Willie Nelson starred as preacher Julian Shay who left Philadelphia for the Montana lowlands with his new bride (Morgan Fairchild). After she leaves him for an old lover because of the restrictions placed on her lifestyle, Shay guns them down and falls from grace. He finds a new life when he meets a widow (Katherine Ross) and her son. The movie was based on a song of the same name that Nelson wrote.

The Strawberry Blonde - A comedy filmed in 1941 about a dentist at the turn of the century who wonders whether he married the right girl. Starring James Cagney, Olivia De Havilland, and Rita Hayworth.

The Red-Haired Alibi - Shirley Temple's first movie in 1932. She was three years old.

The Redheaded Woman (1932) - This film by MGM is a story of a counter girl who marries her boss but has a hard time fitting into his social circle because of her previous position. The movie features Anita Loos, Jean Harlow, Una Merkel, Lewis Stone, and Chester Morris and was written by Katharine Brush.

The Lady With Red Hair - (1940) Produced by Warner Brothers, this drama starred Miriam Hopkins, Alexis Smith and Claude Rains. Directed by Curtis Bernhardt.

The Reformer and the Redhead (1950) Produced by MGM, this movie was about a small town reform candidate who dumps his crooked benefactor and wins the election with the help of the zookeeper's daughter. Stars Dick Powell, June Allyson, David Wayne, and Marvin Kaplan.

The Redhead from Wyoming (1952) starred the beautiful Maureen O'Hara and other stars such as Jack Kelly and Dennis Weaver. It was directed by Lee Sholem.

Those Redheads From Seattle (1953) starred Gene Barry, Rhonda Fleming, and Agnes Moorehead.

The Redheaded Baby (1931) was produced by Warner Brothers and featured Mel Blanc's voice in various characters. Directed by Rudolph Ising.

Other obscure movies about redhaired characters:

The Cowboy and the Redhead - 1951
The Redhead from Manhattan - 1943
Red Beard (Japan) - 1965
The Man Who Loved Redheads - 1955
Assignment Redhead - 1956
The Girl With The Red Hair (Netherlands) - 1981
Redheads (Australian) - 1992

Dancing Redheads

Redheads - A very special musical comedy, "Redheads," opened February 5, 1959 on Broadway.

Gwen Verdon and Richard Kiley starred, and it was directed and choreographed by the late American director Robert Louis Fosse. In favor of the image of redheads, it was the first stage play musical Fosse directed (1959), and it was a huge success. *Redheads* was written by best-selling American author Sidney Sheldon. The critics loved the acting and the dancing, but found the plot as "complicated as a tax return." Nevertheless, the play went on to appear 433 times and closed on March 19, 1960.

The songs were written by Dorothy Fields, who was the first woman to be inducted into the Songwriters Hall of Fame. She also wrote music for "A Tree Grows in Brooklyn," "Mexican Hayride," "By the Beautiful Sea," and "Annie Get Your Gun."

Redheads On Parade - The movie starred Jack Haley, Dixie Lee, John Boles, and Alan Dinehart. The movie was released by Twentieth Century Fox Productions in 1935, and the music was published by Movietone Music Corporation. The song of the same name was written by the late Jay Gorney. (See "Songs")

SONGS

Tangled Up in Red

Early one morning the sun was shining
I was laying in bed
Wondering if she changed at all,
if her hair was still red.
  "Tangled Up in Blue"- Bob Dylan

Red Earl

I thought I was the Duke of Earl
when I made it with a redhead girl
"Keeping the Faith"- Billy Joel

Is She Red, too?

The *Redhaired Man's Wife* (1960) is an obscure song from "Irish Street Ballads" - by M. O'Lochlain

L.A. Red

Rollin' down the Imperial Highway
With a big nasty redhead at my side
Santa Ana winds blowin' hot from the north
And we was born to ride.
  "I Love L.A." - Randy Newman (the music video for the song featured a redhaired model that was placed by the Redheads International club).

Redheads On Parade

Every little mother's daughter rallies to the new crusade
Everywhere you go, everyone you know
is heading for the Redheads on Parade

Every little redhead sorta puts the others in the shade
Everyone forgets the blondies and brunettes,
when they see the Redheads on Parade

They're way above the masses - they're sugar and spice
they're ginger and molasses and everything that's nice
Every little lady oughta rally to the new brigade,
come and get your share - titian up your hair -
get into the Redheads on Parade

It's a redhead letter day in a redhead USA
From Massachusetts to the Golden Gate,
redheads are here to stay
It's the end of the blondes and platinum,
everyone in town's high-hattin' them
Cause they ain't so cold, and they ain't so hot,
and furthermore I'll tell you what
They ain't got nothing that we ain't got
in the Redheads on Parade

Cause they ain't got this, and they ain't got that,
they ain't got nothing beneath their hat
And that's the reason we're going to bat
for the Redheads on Parade!

(Submitted with permission by Gorney's wife, Sandra Gorney)

Tigerlilly
From the album of the same name by Natalie Merchant

"Your pale blue eyes
Your strawberry hair
lips so sweet
skin so fair"

129

TELEVISION

Capitol – Producer Don Sullivan. Brenda Cleeg and her mother are trying to find Brenda a date for her "coming out" party. Her mother mentions a boy's name as a suggestion, to which Brenda replies, "Mother, I can't go out with him - he's a redhead!"

Her mother answered, "Brenda, just because he has redhair doesn't mean you can discriminate against him."

"No, mother, I can't go out with him. His hair would clash with all these dresses that we've picked out," she said coldly.

Trapper John – (aired March 10, 1986 - CBS) Portraying a redhaired, bumbling intern plagued by a ghost in this episode, J.T. (Timothy Busfield), lands himself and Gonzo (Gregory Harrison) in jail. They were arrested for searching a dead surgeon's home while trying to find important notes critically needed for a special medical operation. While they are in jail, Gonzo chastises J.T.

"I must be crazy," Gonzo moans.

"I thought I was the one that was crazy," J.T. replied.

"No, I'm crazy to have listened to a red-haired delinquent... and it lands me in jail," Gonzo mutters dejectedly.

Different Strokes – Arnold (Gary Coleman), the main character of the show is talking to Sam, a little redhaired neighbor boy.

"Go away, Sam," orders Arnold.

"How come?" replied Sam.

"Because this balcony is off limits to redheaded pests." (Big laugh from the audience).

In another scene, Arnold loses a model rocket when it lands in the Russian Embassy. Thinking of ways to retrieve the rocket, Arnold suggests that they send Sam to get it because "his hair matches the color of their flag!"

Bonanza – The popular television series once featured a story about a con man cheating the townfolk of Virginia City out of their money for shares in a "steam car". A main player in this segment was a dance hall girl by the name of "Big Red." During the dialogue of this particular show, the name "Big Red" was stated over 25 times, referring to the dance hall girl character. The show itself was lighthearted and humorous, with a bittersweet ending when "Big Red," a bighearted redhaired girl ended up getting married.

The Andy Griffith Show – As a popular early '60's television series, the Andy Griffith Show had downhome humor and wit.

One show had Barney Fife (Don Knotts) and Andy Taylor (Andy Griffith) trying to convince a character named Henry that he wasn't really a jinx. They organized a party and held a drawing for a door prize that they arranged for Henry to win without his knowledge. Everyone at the party was in on the scheme, which was carried out by having the raffle holders keep quiet when a raffle number was pulled out of a hat and announced. Since all the numbers given out were the same, by keeping quiet, the other players acted like Henry received the winning number.

Everybody waited silently for Henry to jump up and claim the prize. But he just stood there looking dejected. Andy prompted him, "Well, Henry, what number did you get?"

"I got 6 - 7/8," Henry answered. Barney took a look at Henry's number and exclaimed, "Aw, Andy, he pulled out the hat size!"

This really convinced Henry that he was jinxed, but Andy explained to him that everyone in the room had been a part of the plan, because they were his friends and they wanted him to feel better about himself. "The luckiest thing a man could have is his friends," Andy said.

They gave the prize to Henry anyway, and Andy asked Barney to give Henry a ride home. True to his character, Barney was a little nervous about having the "jinxed" Henry in his car. Barney looks around the room nervously, then yells out, "Hey Red!" and rubs the head of a disconcerted young redhaired man who was passing by, thinking that rubbing a redhead's head would ward off bad luck!

Columbo – This episode starring Peter Falk and Richard Basehart (playing the bad guy) had Columbo in England trying to solve a murder. In his trademark closing speech, Columbo reveals the true identity of the murderer. He began by stating: "Remember when you were a little boy in school, and you had to get the attention of the pretty redhaired girl in the front row..." The episode was produced by Dean Hargrove.

Anne of Green Gables – In a PBS television movie based on the book, "Anne of Green Gables," Mrs. Lynde, a gossipy old lady, had gained ill-favor with Anne, who in turn called her "an awful old woman." When Anne apologized later, and attributed her outburst to having redhair, Mrs. Lynde replied, "Don't worry about your hair - when I was a girl - I knew a girl who had redhair every bit as red as yours, but when she grew older - it turned a beautiful shade of dark auburn."

I Call Her Red

My So Called Life – In this much-acclaimed 1995 television series, Jordan, the high school love interest of Angela, the teenage star of the show, surprises her by singing a love song he wrote, "I Call Her Red." Angela has redhair. She falls hopelessly in love with him, but he stands her up. She finds out later that the song was written about his car.

Chapter Ten

TRANSLATIONS

There are many words that mean red or redhaired, and that includes proper names. The following are common names that were derived from their earlier origins as meaning "redhaired". Notice how most of the names start with the letter "R":

FIRST NAMES:

"Reddish-brown haired"
 Roano - (Spanish)

"Little redhaired one"
 Roslin - (Old French)
 Rosslyn or *Rosselin* - (Old English)

"Hair like old iron"
 Russell and *Rusty* - (Saxon)
 Roussel - (French)

"Redhaired"
 Rufus - (Latin);
 Rowan - (Irish - Gaelic)
 Roy - (Celtic)

"Redhaired King; a man whose spirit matches his hair"
 Rory - (Celtic)
 Rurik - (Slavik)
 Ruodrik - (Old German)

LAST NAMES:

"Son of the redheaded man"
   Rowson - (Anglo - Irish),
   Reading - (Old English),
   Ruskin - (Saxon - French)
   Flynn - (Gaelic)

"Redhaired"
   Ruff or *Ruffe* - (French)
   Rowe - (Old English)
   Rowan - (Irish - Gaelic)
   Derry - (Gaelic)
   Rooney - (Irish - Gaelic)
   Rogan - (Irish - Gaelic)
   Reed or *Read* - (Old English)

"Redhaired man"
   Rodman - (Teutonic)

"Of redhair"
   Roth - (Celtic)

"Man whose hair is like a torch"
   Rush - (French)

How About Sunset?

The name "Seynatawnee" means "hair of the Rising Sun" in Cherokee Indian language. In English, the word "tawny" also connotes a color of light brown to brownish orange. [Middle English, from

Anglo-Norman "taune," variant of Old French "tane," from past participle of "taner," to tan(!)]

I Know You are but What Am I?

Nicknames (coming from the early English word "ekename"; "eke" meaning "additional name"), have supplied a multitude of sobriquets that have long been bones in the throats of redheads. The word "redhead" is even a nickname.

Where did the term "redheads" come from? "Redde-haired" was common in the early Middle ages, as was "titian" (named after the popular Italian painter, Titian), but some believe the noun, "red-head", has been possibly linked to the English royal family around the time of King Henry VIII. The theory goes that many members in the English Royal family of the House of Tudor were redheads, and the term may actually have been alluding to the fact that the "Head" of state was redhaired, and it became a nickname for the King, the "red *Head*." Additionally, the color red was always connected with royal ceremonies.

The focus on the word "head" in those days made people swallow nervously, as there were many heads being lopped off during that time, including redhaired Mary, Queen of Scots, who was executed by her cousin, redheaded Queen Elizabeth I.

"Red" origins:
   réad - Old English
   råd - Old Frisian (French)

ród - Old Saxon
rood - Dutch
rót - Old German
roudhos - Old Ireland
rhudd - Welsh
ruadh - Gaelic
rufus - Latin
rad - Serbian

"Hair" origins:
haer, he'r - Old English
har - Old Norse
haire - French

"-Head" - mutated from the form correlating to "head" from "hood", the Old English word, "had," typified leader or covering, possibly in reference to a crown.

"'Ruber crine' - a redde headed felowe"
(Coopers Thesaurus 1565)

Classy Car
The name of the famous and much-desired automobile, the Ferrari *Testarossa*, actually translates directly into English from Italian as "The Red Head."

Parley View, Francie?

Here are how redheads are called in different parts of the world:

Italy	*"Capo rosso"* or *"dai capella rossi,"* *"Testa rossa"*
France	*"rousse," "roux," "rouguin, "roussette"*
Latin	*"rufus"*
Spain	*"de pelo rojo,"* (*rubio* - refers to *red* as gold)
Russian	*"rishij"* (pronounced "ree-zhee" and means "hair like the sun")
Hawaii	*"Ehu"*
Germany	*"Rothaarige"*

"Brunetted" When You're Happy

When you get angry in Scotland, you're referred to as being "redheadit".

Why Not "White" head, Blondie?

The French word "roussette" would be a romantic name for redheads. Because of the possibility of English language having something to do with originating the term "redhead", the French version of redhair, "roussette," may have been overpowered in common English language usage. "Redhead" has lost its strength of respect or romance against the name of "blondes", and "brunettes", both French definitions of hair color. Proper names of "Russell" or "Rusty," actually were derived from "Rousette," which is an accepted name for redheads today in France. Notice that the name "roussette" sounds similar to the English word "russet," which means "having the color of reddish brown."

Those Russians ARE Really Reds!

It can be said that the current nickname for the citizens of Russia, "Reds," so named because of their red flag and emblems, is in actuality an old English translation of the name "Russian."

In an ironic twist of words, redheads have had to endure the insulting statement, "I'd rather be dead than red," which was initially meant to be a slur against communism, but came to be used by some people as a sneering poke directed at redheads.

It seems that Russia, in the beginning of its formation, was a country founded by a redhaired Scandinavian pirate and adventurer named Rurik, which in Slavic means "redhaired King." His Varangian (Viking) warriors were called the "Rus" people, a derivation of the Latin word "russus" which meant "pertaining to red," and the Saxon definition of redhair, "roussel." Rus was used to describe the emerging monarchy and the light-haired people who followed the newly proclaimed redhaired Grand Duke, who probably had plenty of redheads among his Viking hordes. They then formed the Rus Dynasty.

According to Russian emigre/writer/lecturer, Victor Enyutin, a professor at the University of California in Irvine, the Soviet people still refer to themselves as "russkiys" (roos-ski), and that there is no clear meaning to them how that term was derived, as the language has been permeated with European and Serbian dialect over the past ten centuries. The current Russian term for a "redhead," barring spelling translation limitations with the Russian alphabet, is "rishij," (ree-zhee) a metaphor meaning "hair burned by the sun." There is no direct translation because many Russians don't consider red hair to be an actual color of red. Their word for "red" is *ruda*, a derivative of the Gaelic *ruadh*.

Enyutin said that the early Slavic nations, mostly darkhaired, may have referred to the new Norse ruler, Rurik, and his settlers as "Rus" because with the combination of the ruddiness of their skin and their blonde and reddish hair, the term "rus" was a common word used by European traders and the local peoples to describe reddish colors. Thus, the Slavic people assigned the new ruler's dynasty, "Rus," as the translation of the day for "being of the reddish-haired tribe"! The term "Rus" was eventually lengthened to "Russia." The Rus Dynasty ruled for over 700 years during the Dark Ages.

Pure white hair is referred to in Russia as "blondien." Anyone's hair that is redder or browner than this extreme "blondien" hair is usually called "rishij," being that they are more reddish or lighter-haired and light-complexioned than the average Slavic/Serbian person.

Many Russian scholars, however, dispute the claim that the Rus Dynasty was actually started by the Norse Varangians, claiming that the eastern Slavic tribes had already formed a feudal state, and that the

Rus people were a Slavic tribe along the Ros River. Their claim doesn't address how the Ros River, another linguistic reference of the day meaning "Red River," was so named.

To further substantiate the claim that Russia was named for the "reddish-(haired) people," most dictionaries have the word *Russia* placed between the word *russet* (yellowish or reddish), and the word *rust* (reddish brown). Also near those definitions are the words *rubric*, *ruddy* and *rubicund*, all pertaining to the word "red". Even the word *rustle* can be connotated to refer to redheads, as the common opinion in some locales during the 10th century was that redheads were thieves and vagrants *rustling* goods. The phonetic similarities for the word "red" throughout Europe during that period lends credibility to the claim that the name "Russia" can indeed mean "land of the redhaired people." (*See the Bulgarian city "Ruse"*)

Who are the Greenies?

In Australia, redheads are nicknamed "Blueys." Odd name for a redhead, but when you get into a scuffle "Down Under," they call it "getting into a blue." The reference to being "blue" stemmed from the days when Scottish warriors would paint their faces blue before a battle. Since redheads are thought to be hot-tempered, they are nicknamed "blueys!"

TEASING

There have been a plethora of names designed to make redheads see red. Most of them are yelled out in good fun, but many redheads don't think they're funny. Here's the names that we've been able to find.

Firetruck
Sorrel Top ("reddish brown" - the color of a horse)
Red
Match stick
Towering Inferno
Rusty
Woody Woodpecker
Red on the Head
Duracell (the copper-top battery)
Carrot-top
Fire brain
Howdy Doody
Flame-brain
Freckle-Faced Strawberry
Bozo
Corrosive Brain
Pinky
Beet-head
Lobster

Unfriendly Phrases: "Beat him like a redhaired stepchild," "Rather be dead than red on the head," "Red, red, wet the bed."

Redheads have comebacks of their own:
"I'd rather drown in a pond than be a brown or a blonde."

Chapter Eleven

REDHEAD FASHION & BEAUTY TIPS

Colors

Fashion experts say that redheads cannot be predictable. There are many colors redheads can wear. Wear black - and use plenty of blush to bring out the contradiction in colors. Redheads can even wear red, which comes off strong but accessible with white cuffs and collar.

Pink is the color of blush that blends well with redheads. Pastel colors, especially heavy with black highlights above the eyes are nice if your eyes are blue. With that combination, you must wear a light, almost pale coverup, do not wear orange blush. Gold is a special color that adds brilliant highlights to redheads. Wear it sparingly, but obvious.

Jewelry

The desirable jewel for the redhead is the emerald. Redheads do not look good in phony "imitation" jewelry, as it tends to make them look tawdry. Redheads were meant to be classy, regal, and elegant. Get as close to those terms as possible for optimum results. Redheads can carry it off easily. Diamonds with emeralds are devastatingly seductive on a redhead.

Fragrances

Many redheads must be careful about the cologne or perfume they wear, because they lack a subsequent amount of skin oil to make the scent take hold. Also, some floral fragrances can smell odd on the redhead's skin. If you must wear a fragrance that may not take to your skin, here's a simple solution: Wear it in your hair!

Dull the Diamond

For those redheads who may want to dye their hair to a lesser color, they would be best to stay within a slightly darkening or lightening of their own color. Red hair is very hard to change, because of the pigment being so brilliant already and it tends to overpower the dye. The skin tones of a redhead make it difficult for them to become too blonde or too darkhaired, as the contrast would seem obvious.

Skin Care

Redheads tend to have dry and tender skin, so they should drink plenty of water and stay covered up in the sun, either with a hat or sunscreen lotion. Pale complexions are returning to fashion and are expected to stay in fashion indefinitely because of the high incidence of skin cancer being reported in the last ten years. All medical reports have pointed to suntans and the sun to being the number one cause of skin cancer. Tanning is actually a health hazard; its results (brown skin) actually signifies a killing of the skin cells in the epidermis - tan skin is just dead skin cells.

Fair, smooth, skin used to be a very desirable quality in women, but with the advent of tuberculosis during the early 1920's, medical advice was to "get some sun and warm weather." Subsequently, those rich enough began visiting Mexican resorts, Las Vegas, Mediterranean hideaways, Palm Springs, Miami, and other hotspots during cold winter months, and people began associating a tan with health and financial independence. Skin cancer rose to alarming rates.

By the year 2000, many doctors say that popular culture will associate a tan with ignorance. (See "Science")

Chapter Twelve

SCIENCE

REDHEADS: STEREOTYPIC IMAGES
The following is a report on perceived attractiveness of people by hair color. The study was done by Professors DENNIS E. CLAYSON - University of Northern Iowa and MICOL R.C. MAUGHAN - Buena Vista College. Psychological Report. 1986. 59.811-816.) Reprinted with permission.

In a study involving 100 college subjects, blondes had a very positive stereotype. Blonde females were seen as beautiful, pleasant, and extremely feminine. Blonde males were seen as strong, active, pleasant, successful, and good-looking. On the other hand, redheaded females were seen as unattractive, but as competent and professional. Unfortunately, redheaded males had a surprisingly negative stereotype. They were seen as very unattractive, less successful, and rather effeminate. Further cause for dismay is that hair-color stereotypes seem to be very long lasting.

The impetus for the present study was the unusual findings in an attempt at replicating an earlier 1968 study which had shown that the perceived height of a person increased with perceived status. A pilot study was conducted in which a target person was introduced to one group of 13 student subjects as a new professor and to another group of 10 subjects as a student janitor. Thirty minutes after the target person left, the students were asked to recall his physical characteristics. Both groups correctly remembered the target's height within less than 0.2 in. of his actual height, replicating the findings of Lerner and Moore (1974). The finding of interest, however, was that 62% of the "professor" group remembered the target as being blonde and 15% remembered him as a redhead. In the "student janitor" group only 10% remembered him as a blonde and 60% remembered him as a redhead. The target person was a strawberry blonde with a flaming red mustache.

A quick review indicated that hair color has been associated symbolically with personal attributes, but the pattern appears to be mixed. Clowns, Howdy Doody, Lucille Ball, Red Skelton, Red Buttons, and allegedly Judas Iscariot had/have red hair. Marilyn Monroe, Jessica Lange, and Steve Canyon are blondes. But then, Ramses II, Cleopatra, Queen Elizabeth I, and Thomas Jefferson, as well as Ann-Margret were redheads and Hitler was particularly fond of blondes. Nevertheless, the students in the above mentioned study appeared to be sharing a common stereotype based on hair color.

Very few investigations of preference by hair color have been conducted. One study in 1971 found that for all men and women, for 42 comparisons, redheaded men were rated significantly superior on none. In fact. neither dark nor blonde men saw redheaded men as superior on any trait. Women rated redheaded men only as "safe".

Redheaded women were rated slightly better, as being rugged, complex, colorful, and strong willed. One of the researchers on this subject, Professor Lawson, wondered at these results and postulated that they may have been due to the small number of redheads on the campus where the study was conducted (approximately 1.5% were redheads). Two thousand miles away, Feinman and Gill (1978) in a study of physical attractiveness preferences, found that only 7% of men and 2% of women preferred red hair, while only 1% of men and 2% of women disliked blonde hair.

The authors asked, "Why is there such a tremendous aversion to redheads?" Possibly, they suggest, there are negative stereotypes associated with red hair. The present study was designed to study possible blonde-red hair stereotypes and to answer Feinman and Gill's question. The environment from which the subjects were drawn also contained approximately four times more redheads (6%) and two times more Blondes (28%) than were found in Lawson's study, allowing a test of his proposition that negative red-head stereotypes were due to the absence of relevant models.

Results

As an example, the closest concept of interest to feminine was blonde. In comparison to blonde, the concept of a female redhead was seen as 5.3 times further from the concept of feminine as the concept of a blonde female. On the other hand, a blonde male was seen as 1.23 times further from feminine than a redheaded male. For both the male and female redheads, the distance to neutrality was closer than for blondes. The redheaded female is clustered very closely to the professional concepts of doctor and professor. The blonde female clusters with the concept of feminine.

The redheaded male was placed closer to janitor and fool and further from doctor than the blonde male concept. Blonde females were rated as significantly more beautiful and feminine than redheaded females.

Overall, blonde females were evaluated generally more positively, and blonde males were rated significantly more positively.

A correlational analysis showed that the stereotypes of blondes (both men and women) worsened with the age of the respondent. Redheaded women were seen more favorably with age, but redheaded men had significant correlations between the increasing age of the respondents and being sad, feminine, unpleasant, weak, slow, and shallow.

To evaluate further the redheaded men's negative image, 14 additional students of mixed racial and ethnic backgrounds were asked to complete differentials on the concepts blonde, dark haired (Anglo), black (Negro), Chicanos, and American Indian (all male concepts). Rated as most to least beautiful in order were: blonde, dark, black, Chicano, Indian, and then redhead. Blonde, dark and black men were rated significantly more beautiful than redheads. Of the six concepts, redheaded men were rated the weakest and the most feminine.

Discussion

Redheaded women were seen as a relatively more powerful professional type. rather no-nonsense and not physically attractive. Their blonde sisters were stereotyped as beautiful, pleasant, pleasing, and extremely feminine. Blonde men were seen as strong, active, pleasant, successful and good-looking. The redheaded man has a surprisingly negative stereotype, being seen as very unattractive, less successful, and rather effeminate, with less potency than even the redheaded woman.

Redheads may have such a negative stereotype because they are relatively rare. Very little data on the proportions of hair color in the Caucasian population is available. Lawson reported that 22% of his female sample was blonde (19% real, 3% dyed). One of the present authors, as part of a study of the use of female models in advertising, recorded the hair color of about 200 women passing a set location in public places in each of seven American cities. Excluded from the total sample were non-Caucasians, women with gray hair, and hair colors that could not be easily differentiated. The undifferentiated accounted for about 12% of the sample and consisted mostly of hair colors between blonde and brown. The total usable sample was 1,298. Blondes accounted for 25.7% of the total, 57.2% were brown-haired, 11% had black hair, and only 6% were redheads. Preliminary surveys of males have so far indicated about the same proportions. With fewer redheads than lefthanders, redheads may simply be relatively unknown to many persons, but this still does not explain why red hair is seen so negatively and why red hair is used to portray villains and fools. (The movie "Dune" is a good example.)

Redheads have an abnormal pigmentation pattern that leads to increased sensitivity not only to light. but also to bruising and pain. Freckles, which may be the result of UV-induced somatic mutation, and high incidence of birth marks which may be the result of intrauterine somatic mutations, are almost universal among redheads.

Redheads also seem to be more susceptible to medullary cystic disease of the kidneys and juvenile diabetes, Redheads may be seen as unattractive because they display phenotypical expressions of poor health. Jung has proposed that this tendency may be inherited and therefore universal. Unfortunately for this hypothesis, the inheritance of red hair appears to be quite complex since most or all humans may be carriers of red genes. Further, no evidence has been found that any pure biological determinant, except sex, has any reliable impact on human assortative mating patterns.

Guthrie (1976) has suggested that women, in cultures where it has been acceptable, have dyed their hair blonde because the light blonde hair gives them a child-like appearance, that is, the appearance of an attractive subordinate. The stereotype may be of long standing, especially in Europe. Ancient Greek actors used black wigs for villains, blonde for heroes, and red wigs for the clown or fool, when it may be true that the color red itself has negative connotations associated with a person. The average redhead may not be so attractive to a society that attributes lightness (with a tan) to femininity and darkness to masculinity. A person may simply not be that attractive with very light skin, no tan, and freckles, combined with an unusual hair color.

Redheads can take solace, however, from knowing that red hair comes in and out of fashion. Red hair has been especially popular during periods of romance and renaissance. It becomes almost a challenge to not find a redheaded angel or madonna in painting during the period of Raphael. A casual sample of 122 post-Raphaelite paintings from centuries later showed 63.1% of the women portrayed as redheads and of the major characters, 79.2% were redheads. Then there are those, regardless of the age, who have simply loved red hair, persons of talent like Titian, Monet and Renoir, and more average souls like the present authors.

BURNING ISSUE OF SKIN CANCER

"The problem is that we associate being tanned with being healthy. It's not true, especially for fair-complexioned people." - Dr. Donald L. Morton, Director of the John Wayne Cancer Clinic.

Skin cancer is a frightening possibility for many redheads, and those who refuse to acknowledge the existence of such a disease are putting themselves into the uppermost of the high-risk category of which they already belong. The large majority of skin cancer patients are of Scandinavian, Scottish, and Northern European descent. The reasons for this seem to be because redhaired and fair-skinned people produce a small amount of *melanin*, a chemical released by the body that helps create pigment to protect itself from the sun's burning rays.

It is estimated that over 30,000 new cases of cutaneous melanoma and 6,500 deaths from this disease were recorded in the United States in 1991. The occurrence of melanoma in this country is rising at the rate of 4% each year. This is becoming the most common cancer, except for lung cancer among women, according to the National Cancer Institute.

Melanoma is a much more prevalent disease among fair-skinned people than people with more pigmented skin (such as Blacks, Hispanics, or Asians), making the death rate among whites higher. In the United States, the incidence among whites increased by almost 70 percent from 1972 to 1987 . The yearly rate of death from melanoma among whites is approximately 10 per 100,000 individuals.

It should be noted that most new cases of melanoma are diagnosed early and can be cured by surgery. The overall 5-year relative survival rate is high for patients with localized melanoma (91%).

Ignoring diagnosis or failing to diagnose the disease in time can be damaging. When the disease has spread to other sites in the area of the original cancer, the 5-year survival rate lowers to 50 percent, and where the cancer has spread to distant sites in the body, the rate of survival is a low 14 percent.

We do not know what causes melanoma, but several risk factors have been recognized, and one of them is ultraviolet radiation (UV).

Exposure to UV radiation from the sun and other sources has been determined to be the major cause of melanoma and other skin cancers. Only a fraction of the sun's UV radiation (solar radiation) reaches the Earth's surface, and most of it is contained by the atmosphere's ozone layers. The amount of UV radiation reaching the Earth decreases with distance (latitude) away from the Equator and increases at higher altitudes.

United States has seen a steady rise in cancer over the past 50 years, during which time Americans have engaged in more outdoor recreational activities, placed more emphasis on tanning, scantier clothing, and a growing shift of the population to warm, sunny climates. Environmental conditions such as heat, wind, season, time of day, and physical surroundings (even snow, sand, or water can also greatly increase exposure because they reflect UV radiation).

Scientists believe that the atmosphere's ozone layer is thinning and may eventually weaken to let more UV radiation to reach the earth and increase even more the risk of melanoma. The ozone layer is being depleted by chlorofluorocarbons, such as Freon, which are man-made substances. In the past, these chemicals served as propellants in aerosol sprays, and they are still used in refrigerators and air conditioners.

Other Risk Factors

Although the sun-exposed areas of the body, such as the arms and legs, head, neck, and upper extremities are at the greatest risk, these areas don't account for all cases of melanoma.

It is possible that other risk factors also play a role in the development of melanoma. Melanoma also commonly occurs on the main body in men, a site that is not routinely exposed to UV radiation. Melanoma risk is also greater in people with variable intense sun exposure, such as office workers on vacation in sunny locations such as the beach, than in outdoor workers with constant exposure to the sun.

According to the National Cancer Institute:

1.   People who are protected from UV radiation by naturally dark skin have the lowest rates of melanoma; however, they are not totally protected from the condition.

2.   People who have **red** or blond hair, **fair skin, freckles,** and **blue** eyes and who **sunburn easily** but rarely tan **are at greater risk for developing melanoma.** The incidence is highest among fair-skinned people living near to the Equator, where the UV radiation exposure is greatest.

3.   The risk is higher than average for people who were severely sunburned as children.

4.   Those persons with xeroderma pigmentosum, a rare hereditary disease in which the skin and eyes are extremely sensitive to light, are much more likely than the general population to develop melanoma.

5.   Individuals with very large nevi: "Nevi" is the medical term for moles, which are clusters of melanocytes. Individuals with very large nevi (20 centimeters, or 7.8 inches, in diameter) that are present from birth have a higher-than-average risk of developing melanoma.

6.   People with certain types of atypical nevi may have an increased risk for this disease. Atypical nevi are generally larger than ordinary moles and have irregular borders that fade into the surrounding skin.

Moles (atypical nevi)

Moles may play an important part in detecting the cancer early. Moles may be flat, or have parts that may be raised above the skin surface. Their color is not usually uniform and may be dark brown, some times with pink or reddish areas. While some people have more than 100 unusual moles on their skin, the average adult has 10 to 40 moles.

It is important to remember that although people with atypical nevi may have increased risk for melanoma, most do not develop this disease. The chance of developing melanoma is greatest for persons with many such nevi who are also from melanoma-prone families (i.e., in which two or more relatives—parents, children, brothers, sisters—have had melanoma).

It's obvious that people with atypical nevi should avoid too much sun exposure. An examination by a doctor on a regular schedule, especially those from families with multiple cases of melanoma, is highly recommended.

Removal of stable atypical nevi does not assure immunity to getting melanoma, because it can still develop in normal skin.

Still, sun exposure remains the major cause of melanoma of the skin. The harmful effects of sun exposure begins in childhood. Severe sunburn as a child is associated with an increased risk of developing melanoma later in life. Limiting sun exposure is the most effective plan to decrease the risk of developing melanoma. During the summertime, many people can be burned by the sun after only 30 minutes of continuous exposure.

Throughout the summer months, UVB radiation exposure can be reduced by staying out of the sun between 10 a.m. and 3 p.m A simple test to see how dangerous the sun is for people at risk for skin cancer is the "shadow method," which basically is done by looking at your shadow. It your shadow is short, not elongated, then your chance for exposure is great. This "shadow method" works for any location and at any time of year. It is based on the principle that the closer the sun comes to being directly overhead, the stronger are its UV rays.

However, be aware that the harmful effects of UV radiation exposure are cumulative and each person's tolerance varies under their own personal sensitivities.

Protections and Safeguards

When you have to be in the sun, wearing protective clothing (such as a hat and long sleeve shirt) and using a sunscreen lotion are especially important. Sunscreens are rated in strength from 2 to 30 or higher sun protection factor (SPF). The U.S. Food and Drug Administration (FDA) requires that this rating, be printed on the sunscreen dispenser. The higher the SPF rating, the greater the blockage of UV radiation. There are studies continuing on the benefits of ratings higher than 15 SPF.

Sunscreens should be applied about 30-60 minutes before each sun exposure and should be reapplied after swimming or perspiring heavily. People should not be comfortable thinking that they are safer on overcast days, because a person can still be exposed to substantial UV radiation (about 80 percent as much as on a clear day).

Some medications, such as antibiotics and antidepressants, can make the skin especially sensitive to sunlight. People taking such medications should check with their physician before tanning, either indoors or outside.

There are artificial sources of UV radiation such as tanning lamps used at home or in tanning salons. The FDA warns that these can be as dangerous as sun exposure and that people burn easily and hardly tan should also not think that these lights are safe. Even those people who feel they tan easily should be careful in a tanning salon.

Signs and Symptoms of Melanoma

Melanoma can start in an existing mole or as a new, mole-like growth. If detected early, it can be usually cured with effective treatment. Moles that have or that develop any of the following characteristics should be examined by a physician as soon as they are noticed:

1. Multiple colors: Melanomas tend to have a variety of colors (red, white, blue, and sometimes black or dark brown) within a single mole.

2. Large size: Melanomas generally are at least 5 millimeters (mm) across (about 1/4 inch). If there is an increase (gradual or sudden) in the size of a mole, it may be a melanoma.

3.   Irregular border: Melanomas are likely to have uneven or notched borders.

4.   Abnormal surface: A mole may be a melanoma if it is scaly, flaky, oozing, or bleeding or has an open sore that does not heal.

5.   Unusual texture: If a mole feels hard or lumpy, it may be a melanoma.

6.   Abnormal skin around a mole: If pigment (color) from a mole has spread to surrounding skin, or if nearby skin is red or swollen or loses its pigmentation (becomes white or gray), a melanoma may be present.

7.   Change in appearance of the skin: Melanomas may develop as new pigmented spots in a skin area that had been normal.

8.   Unusual sensation. A mole may be a melanoma if it itches or is painful or tender.

Diagnosing Melanoma – An experienced physician, especially a dermatologist, can often identify a melanoma on sight, although a biopsy is the only sure way to make a diagnosis.

A biopsy is the surgical removal of tissue for microscopic examination by a pathologist. The pathologist determines whether the tissue is cancerous, and, if so, whether it is a basal or squamous cell carcinoma or a melanoma. A biopsy usually can be done in the doctor's office under local anesthesia.

If melanoma is diagnosed, the physician conducts additional tests to determine the stage of the disease. The staging of melanoma gives the doctor information about the depth to which the cancer has entered the skin and subcutaneous tissue, how widely it has spread, and whether it has metastasized.

There is a classification system that groups melanomas into five levels based on the deepest layer of skin that has been invaded:

• Level I: The cancer involves only the epidermis (outer skin layer). Characterized by the abnormal growth of cells, it is sometimes called melanoma-in-situ.

• Level II: Melanoma reaches into the papillary dermis (upper portion of the dermis).

• Level III: Cancer extends to the bottom of the papillary dermis.

• Level IV: Melanoma has invaded the reticular dermis (lower part of the dermis).

• Level V: Cancer has penetrated through the layers of the skin into the underlying tissue.

Melanomas are classified into three stages: localized disease (stage I), regional metastasis (stage II), and distant metastasis (stage III).

Treatment Options for Melanoma

Treatment of melanoma that has not spread beyond the original area of growth (especially if it is thin and has not invaded the papillary dermis) is highly effective, and most of these cancers can be cured.

In some cases, melanoma that has spread to nearby lymph nodes also can be treated effectively. At present, however, therapy for melanoma that has spread to distant parts of the body is unsatisfactory, and many scientists are conducting basic research and clinical trials (treatment studies) to find better forms of treatment.

Doctors may recommend one or a combination of several treatment approaches:

1. Surgery
2. Chemotherapy
3. Biological therapy
4. Radiation therapy

Surgery

Most patients with melanoma are treated with surgery. When the tumor is thin and has not spread beyond the initial area of growth (stage I), it is usually curable with surgery alone. Usually, the doctor removes the growth and a small section of normal tissue around it to eliminate any cancer cells that may have spread from the tumor. Researchers have found that removing some healthy tissue surrounding the cancer is necessary to prevent recurrence.

Because it is more likely that larger tumors have begun to spread, wide excision (the removal of a large margin of tissue around a melanoma) is used to treat some stage IB melanomas as well as all stage II and stage III melanomas. A skin graft may be necessary following wide surgical excision.

Depending upon the location of the melanoma and results of the staging evaluation, surgeons sometimes recommend removing regional lymph nodes with a stage IB or stage II tumor. Because regional lymph nodes are often the first sites to which melanomas spread, removing the nodes may reduce the risk of recurrence.

To date, however, no study has shown that removing regional lymph nodes makes a statistically significant difference in the length of time stage IB and stage II patients remain disease free or in the length of their survival.

Chemotherapy

Some melanoma patients treated with surgery still are at a high risk of disease recurrence. Further treatment researchers are evaluating is the use of chemotherapy to kill undetectable cancer cells that remain in the body after surgery.

A treatment known as "isolated limb perfusion" or "arterial perfusion," allows patients to receive high doses of anticancer drugs to only the affected limb. As a result, the patient does not experience many of the side effects that are common with systemic chemotherapy.

Biological Therapy

Biological therapy, also know as biotherapy or immunotherapy, is another important procedure for cancer treatment. It uses tools of modern molecular biology, immunology, and genetics. Biological therapy acts either directly against the cancer or indirectly to change the way the patient's body reacts to a tumor.

It may strengthen the ability of a cancer patient's immune system to fight the growth of cancer cells, or make a cancer cell more susceptible to elimination by the patient's immune system.

A vaccine made up of irradiated, melanoma cells, sometimes in combination with the bacterium called BCG (bacillus Calmette-Guerin), is one form of immunotherapy under investigation. The purpose of this treatment is to sensitize the immune system, which increases its ability to destroy melanoma cells.

Other immunotherapy for melanoma involves interferons, proteins formed by human cells to help regulate certain cell processes. Interferons also have shown some effectiveness in the treatment of some types of melanoma.

These proteins appear to work both by boosting the body's immune reaction to invading cancer cells and by acting directly on cancer cells. Interferons may inhibit the growth of cancer cells or promote their development into cells with more normal behavior.
In similar research, scientists have begun studying the cancer fighting potential of a specific type of white blood cell. These cells, commonly called tumor infiltrating lymphocytes (TIL), can, after leaving the bloodstream, invade tumors and kill cancer cells.

Radiation Therapy
Radiation therapy may be used to treat local recurrences of melanoma that cannot be surgically removed. Radiation therapy has also been tested for its

effectiveness in preventing local recurrences. Unfortunately, such treatment does not appear to improve long-term survival, according to the National Institutes of Health. In cases in which the disease has spread to the lung, gastrointestinal tract, bone, or brain (stage IV), radiation may provide relief from such symptoms as pain.

Prevention and Follow-up

Because certain individuals, especially **redheads**, are at high risk for the development of melanomas and sometimes for recurrence, they should stay out of the sun as much as possible, regularly examine their skin, and at least once a year be examined by a physician (more if you've already had an occurrence of melanoma).

Every redhead person and parents of redhaired children should do their utmost in protecting themselves and their children from the sun's harmful rays. The dangers from skin cancers and other melanomas are very real in the lives of the redhaired.

✳✳✳✳✳✳✳✳✳✳✳✳✳✳✳✳✳✳✳✳✳✳✳✳✳✳✳✳

**"If you don't get out of this fire,
you'll be a redhead."**
(Fredric March to Veronica Lake in the 1947 movie "I Married A Witch," after she asked him how he liked her blonde hair)

Redhanded

According to an informal study done by a prison correctional officer, R. Laurence Taylor, most redhead convicts are green-eyed and of Slavic descent.

Musical Scents

The skin of the redhead has been reported through the ages as having an inability to hold a fragrance, and to having a sweetly musk-like odor of its own. The body chemistry of redheads is said to change continually with their emotions, so perfumes and colognes are always changing scents when applied to their skin. Much experimentation is usually required for the redhead to find a suitable and stable scent to wear.

Color Blind

In 1978, two professors conducted a survey among 1000 students at the campus of the University of Wyoming. They were trying to find certain attributes that figured in the sexual attractions and preferences of the students. In the category of hair color, less than 2% of the results signified a desire for redheads as mates.

HAIR

What is redhair?   Why are there redheads? Scientists don't know the exact answer to those questions, but they have a general idea of what causes redhair.   Let's start with an analysis of hair itself.   A hair strand is made up of three distinct regions:

1.   The cuticle, which is the outermost layer which looks like scales under a microscope and provides protection from the elements.

2.   The cortex, which is the major portion of the hair containing pigment and oil pockets giving hair its color and sheen.

3.   The medulla, which is the innermost layer, but not present in all hair, especially the arm and leg hair (*lanugo*) hair.

The main proponents of hair are protein and moisture.   There are 21 amino acids in hair protein and they account for 64 to 95 per cent of the weight of hair.   Moisture is in the remaining part of the hair, except for 9% of fatty acids.   There are trace elements which make up less than 1% of your hair, and these particles provide a window into the health of a person. Within these trace elements, doctors can ascertain a lack of certain minerals and suggest new diets to correct the deficiency.   As many as 25 elements have been isolated in hair strands, including gold, aluminum, selenium and calcium.

Hair growth begins in a minute structure called the *follicle*. Each follicle grows out of the inner layer of skin, or *dermis*, in a slanted fashion, which causes the "lay" of the hair. Cowlicks occur because of follicle whorls colliding with one another. When the follicle pattern is symmetrical, the hair is easier to part.

Hair Follies

Each hair follicle contains a network of nerves, and a muscle named the *arrectores pilorum*. This muscle is a unit of the involuntary nervous system. When it gets cold or when a person expresses fear, it contracts and creates "goose bumps." The involuntary nerves also control the workings of the *sebaceous* sacs surrounding each follicle. These sacs create a substance called *sebum* which coats the hair strand, lubricating it as it grows through the *epidermis*. Dry hair in winter is a result of cold weather diminishing the sebum output.

The hair follicle is thickest at the base, where it expands into a bulb. During hair growth, cells continually divide at the base of the bulb and move up the narrower tip, where they elongate and align themselves vertically. Inside the bulb are blood vessels called the *dermal papilla* which supply the energy and oxygen needed for hair growth. Although cell division no longer occurs past the tip of the bulb and is considered dead beyond that point, the hair does not harden for one-third of the way up the follicle.

The interior of the follicle acts as a sheath and determines hair texture. The sheath for straight hair is mainly circular; wavy hair is oval and kinky hair is convex. After the hair cells harden, the sheath cells are discarded and disposed of by enzyme action.

The hair continues to grow up the follicles at the rate of 35 millimeters a day, or an inch every six weeks. Although it can last over a long period of time, hair growth is not continuous. The follicle goes through a distinct cycle of rest, growth and transition.

In the resting phase, there is no cell division and the sides of the bulb shrink and press against the hair shaft, which has developed microscopic "spears" to anchor it firmly. When a growth cycle begins, the follicle is pushed downward from the old strand and forms the nucleus for the generation of a new hair. The new hair strand forms and dislodges the old hair within the follicle. The old shaft becomes dislodged and falls out.

Hair grows at an even rate until it reaches its maximum length of several feet. Then it develops the miniature "arrowheads" to set in the dermis. The follicle deteriorates rapidly and again begins its resting cycle. Scientists have not figured out why this cycle, which allows human scalp hair to grow continuously for up to 20 years, occurs. A person's hormones, general health, and nutrition can dictate the speed in which their hair grows.

Color It Red

There is a great variety of colors, shades and tints of hair, but only two chemically distinct pigment granules have been isolated--*eumelanin* for dark hair; and *pheomelanin* for light hair. The production of these two agents and the densities in which they occur is genetically controlled, and bring about all the different shades of hair color in existence. The two color elements are formed by the blending of enzymes and amino acids in pigment cells called *melanocytes*.

The melanocytes lie dormant at the base of the hair follicle until it begins its phase of active growth. At that point, activity increases and pigment granules, measuring about .15 microns in diameter, are formed. These granules are then gathered by the cell into tightly rounded bundles and transferred to the cortical area of the newly forming hair shaft. The granules then disperse and by the time the hair shaft leaves the scalp it has attained its true color. When hair turns gray or white, it is due to the failure of enzyme action in the melanocytes, which is irreversible.

Redhair takes on different tints and even different colors on different parts of the body. It's fairly common for a brown-haired man to have a red beard, and many redheads have blonde eyebrows and body hair. If the redhaired gene carries significant amounts of melanin, (the pigment found in hair and skin cells) the redhair gene will be obscured and the person will be brown or black-haired. As this level of melanin drops, the red shades in a person's hair will become more evident.

Most redheads have fair-skin (a sign of a lack of melanin, since melanin is responsible for the ability to tan). This also answers many ill-referred assumptions as to why a child is born with redhair to parents who are not redheads.

Tyrosine for the Bean

The key amino acid is *tyrosine*, which appears more predominately in darkhaired people than in light. The amount of tyrosine in a person's body has a lot to do with hair color and behavior because of tyrosine's impact on the way the brain works.

Pediatrician Lendon Smith found that in studies of 8,000 hyperactive children, a large percentage of them were redheads. He theorized that *tyrosine*, a genetically regulated amino acid that modifies pigmentation and also helps build neurotransmitters, is directed more towards affecting the neurotransmitters when there is little pigmentation.

Tyrosine is also an important regulator of glucose in the bloodstream, which may explain why certain diets seem to aid in the lessening of hyperactive children. Dr. Smith believes that more tyrosine may be directed towards "hyping up" (redhaired) children, as the tyrosine is augmenting the child's neurotransmitters without the melanin to control it.

In a similar study discussed in the July 1980 issue of *Reader's Digest*, an Israeli researcher believed that there might be some truth in the folk wisdom in many cultures that redheaded people may be a bit temperamental. Psychiatrist Michael Bar of Israel's Shalvata Center reported in a study showing that redheaded children are three to four times more likely than others to develop "hyperactive syndrome." More than two thirds of the children being studied who were hyperactive were redheads.

"It is possible," he says, "that the assumed national characteristics of certain ethnic groups, like the adventurousness of the Vikings and the temperament of the Irish are connected to the high frequency of redheads among them." The redhaired gene is prevalent in many people, but the right environment has to be present in the cell-creation of life in order to produce a true-blue, obvious redhead.

What's the *Trick?*

In 1945, Dr. Peter Flesch and Dr. Stephen Rothman, two doctors at the University of Chicago, experimented to what special chemical qualities pertained to red hair. They collected clippings from barbers' red-haired customers and analyzed over two pounds of hair. Flesch and Rothman found a chemical in the pigment which was a very complex iron compound that they named *trichosiderin*. Although lacking melanin, redheads have an overabundance of *trichosiderin*, which is an elusive, exclusive chemical found in redheads, and not found in any other hair color. Trichosiderin is a special compound made partly of iron, and the agent for giving redheads their lustrous color.

From 100 grams of bright red hair, only 40 milligrams of trichosiderin was isolated. The process of dissolving out the trichosiderin did not change the color of the hair, but it did cause it to lose its lustre. Flesch and Rothman reasoned that the trichosiderin somehow modifies or oxidizes pigment granules without being changed itself. Studies by other researchers determined that trichosiderin appears in varying amounts between all the different shades of red hair. It acts as a unifying link for the various tints.

Understanding all these special circumstances that must exist for a redhead to be born point to the rare and exclusive individuality that redheads possess.

Dyeing To Be Red

Throughout history, red hair as been attained by choice from applying the paste obtained from *henna* (lawsonia inermis), a shrub that grows in the Middle East and India. The red dye from henna is made by shredding the leaves and twigs of the plant and crushing them into powder and stirring the residue in hot water. The paste is applied to the hair and left to set overnight. The red tint that occurs lasts for several weeks. Henna is also thought to have mystical qualities in the more remote areas of the Middle East.

A mixture of henna and coriander seed is thought to keep away the evil eye, along with malevolent spirits called the *jinn*. Icons painted with henna is believed to have spiritual power, and the Prophet Mohammed is said to have dyed his beard with the substance, giving it a conspicuous character consequently bringing about the Arab phrase "by the Prophet's Beard."

What's Your Sign?

According to astrologer Elizabeth Greenwood, the Zodiac creates a whole spectrum of redheads influenced by the following astrological factors according to their time at birth:

Goldie Locks: The Leo-Sun, Sunrise
Pinkie: The Cancer-Moon factor, usually midday
Copper Penny: The Venus-Taurus-Libra factor
Red: The Mars-Aries-Scorpio factor.

Carrot-top: The Mercury-Gemini-Virgo factor
Rusty: The Jupiter-Sagittarius-Pisces factor.
Auburn: The Saturn-Capricorn-Aquarius factor.

These factors include the Sign or planet on the Eastern horizon at the time of birth or the time of day such as Sunrise, Sunset, or Midday.

Martians - From the Red Planet

UC Berkeley astrologers Judith Hill and Jacalyn Thompson investigated the ancient belief that Mars, (traditional red planet of anger, war, and passion) is often prominent in the astrological charts of redhaired people. Beginning with a preliminary test group consisting of the birth times of 100 redheads, several tests were performed to judge the relative strength of Mars in each birth chart. These tests were based on traditional methods, long in favor among astrologers for the accurate judging of birth charts.

These same surveys were also performed on a randomly selected control group consisting of birth charts of 100 non-redheads. Initial results show that the charts of the redheads feature a strongly placed Mars two to five times more frequently (depending on which test) than do the charts of non-redhaired people.

Red Region

Redheads are found more in the uppermost, cool regions of Europe because the less sun required less melanin formation in the body. Through genetic selection over the centuries, the lack of melanin in the body gave way to the redhaired producing gene.

Wallflowers Not!

From an article in the August 25, 1928 issue of "Literary Digest" comes a revelation about why redheads may be considered hot tempered.

"For long enough, observes the "Manchester Guardian", there has been a popular belief that redhair is the sign of an ardent character, and that the head that bears it displays at once the native hue of resolution."

The above excerpt goes on to say that the belief that redheads are hotheaded is an incorrect one and that most redheads are the victims of an inferiority complex. Being teased at school in their youth about their bright hair color has caused most redheads to go either offensive or defensive quite dramatically.

According to this article, if only King William Rufus, Barbarossa, and Queen Elizabeth I had been left alone or admired in their youth for their flaming locks, they would have been mild and complacent monarchs. The article continues by saying that the Barbarossa family was literally a gang of corsairs, plundering and harassing the Christians as much as they could find them. How would history be changed had not these powerful and resolute rulers been teased in their youth about their redhair? How many pages of history would have been deleted if the "ill-judged jests" not "lighted the torches of rebellion in lives that were otherwise peaceful and sedentary?"

After all this time, things should have changed, *"as redhair is admirable in women and certainly no drawback to a man. But it may be that esthetic theodes make slower progress in the young, and that in the matter of simple facts and ancient prejudices, the schoolroom is your true home of lost causes."*

It is a common theory today that redheads and their personality traits had much to contribute through the course of human events because of their adventuresome hyperactivity.

Sere-ous People!

The Roman historian Pliny wrote around 60 A.D. that a people called Seres were essential in maintaining silk trade between Europe and the Far East. He wrote, "The Seres are of more than average height; they have red hair, blue eyes and harsh voices, and have no language in which to communicate their thoughts" (they didn't speak Latin).

Red Turf

During the time of 100 B.C., a group of tribes called the "Turfanese" were described by Chinese historians as "blue-eyed and red-haired." The Turfanese preferred to fight instead of trade, and were eventually conquered by the western Chinese peoples.

Vikings - The Redheads Heritage

Around 900 A.D., powerful men with fair skin and reddish hair and beards invaded Western Europe from the North. They arrived in long wooden ships and created such fear that the townspeople routinely fled to the medieval churches and chanted the prayer "*A furore Normannorum, livera nos Domine* – "From the fury of the Northmen, O Lord, deliver us!" As fearless explorers and traders, the Vikings spread their redhaired genes throughout Europe, North America, and even into the Mediterranean. Iban Fadlan, an Arab scribe, wrote that the Vikings were "as tall as date-palms and all redhaired." In the Far East, the lure of the riches of trade brought Vikings down the Volga and Dneiper Rivers to reach the city of Constantinople, a major trading hub. Their routes were soon established by trade centers they set up along the way, forming the seeds of cities such as Kiev and Novrogod. (See "Russia").

It's easily apparent that the Vikings and other red-haired cultures had more influence on the course of civilization than just the raping and pillaging of towns and countrysides. They made communications through trade and caused massive changes through warfare, and with their settling amongst the indigenous peoples helped create new kingdoms and cultures. Their redheadedness left a legacy that is apparent among many countries even today.

Chapter Thirteen

FICTIONAL CHARACTERS

Ariel - The youngest of King Triton's mermaid daughters from the Walt Disney story, "The Littlest Mermaid." Ariel disobeyed her father by going to the surface of the ocean where she lost her "sea legs" or flippers. As the star in the animated musical, Ariel has become one of the most popular Disney characters.

Nancy Drew - The "new" Nancy Drew, of the famous Nancy Drew book series, is now a "trendy redhead," and is described as having "reddish blonde hair." She uses her wits and charm to solve crimes. Written by a group of writers going by the name of Carolyn Greene.

Pippi Longstockings - Pippi is the child heroine that possessed superhuman strength in the popular children's book of the same name.
Written by Astrid Lindgren, the Pippi Longstocking books featured the adventures of this pigtailed redhead who lives alone with her horse and monkey. Pippi was the delight of her two friends, who were constantly amazed at her strength and never-ending curiosity that always sent them on an adventure.

Raggedy Ann - A stuffed doll with red yarn hair, Raggedy Ann also has a brother with redhair, Raggedy Andy. Very popular, they are well recognized by most countries of the world as characters in children's stories espousing good manners and kindness.

Yosemite Sam - A short, loud-talking, swaggering scoundrel featured in Bugs Bunny cartoons and other animated films by Warner Brothers. He was always having trouble with Bugs Bunny or Daffy Duck, usually losing to either or both of them. His gravelly voice was done by the famous vocal impersonator, Mel Blanc. Yosemite Sam is easily recognizable by his huge red handlebar mustache and oversized hat. Favorite saying: "Ooooo, I HATE that crrrazy rabbit!"

Little Orphan Annie - First appearing in newspapers in the 1930's, Little Orphan Annie was constantly getting into trouble and ultimately being rescued by Daddy Warbucks (the richest man in the world), who was her adopted father. Created by Harold Gray, the comic strip is a continuing saga of her foibles with danger, the suspense building up in each of her episodes. Looking rather wooden, with hollow eyes and straight limbs, Annie says phrases like "leapin' lizards" and "gee whiskers." Her dog Sandy just mutters "Arf."

A movie was made, "Annie," with the part of Annie played by a non-redhead by the name of Aileen Quinn (she wore a redhaired wig). The movie was inspired by a long running broadway play of the same name.

Brenda Starr - Created in 1940 by Dale Messick, Brenda Starr was a reporter always hopping to the four corners of the earth to get a sensational story. Her love life was invariably teetering with one handsome suitor after another, while in search for her one true love, Basil St. John (who suffered from some odd disease and stayed out of reach in whereabouts unknown to Miss Starr).

Hagar the Horrible - A redbearded and redheaded comic strip character, Hagar is a Viking leader surrounded by a nagging wife and bumbling warriors. The strip is written and drawn by Dik Brown. One caption had Hagar's wife placing a smelly charm around his neck. When Hagar complained, his wife replied, "It'll ward off evil spirits, plague, demons, devils, monsters and all dangers .... including flashy redheads!" Syndicated by King Features, it remains a popular strip today.

Uriah Heep - A character in Charles Dickens' "David Copperfield," Mr. Heep was always referring to his "umble self." He was the clerk and later partner of Mr. Wickfield, David's employer, and possessed a sleazy hypocritical composure that gave David the creeps. He was later found out for his misdeeds and was sent to jail.

Becky Sharp - She was the brilliant, beautiful, and amoral redhead heroine in the book *Vanity Fair.*

Red Sonja - Comic book heroine who lives in the age of Conan the Barbarian, a comic book hero who protected the weak in the mythical time of ancient warriors. A movie was made in 1985 about "Red Sonja - She Devil" and the starring part was played by Bridgette Nilsson.

Alfred E. Neuman - The goofy-looking gap-toothed character on the cover of "MAD" magazine, Alfred's motto closely resembles that of all redheads: "What, me worry?"

Alfred E. Neuman was actually named after the Hollywood music director Alfred Newman. The name was used by Mad magazine for several years before it was actually given to the character's face.

Alfred's face was initially a drawing used as far back as 1880, where he appeared in an advertisement for a dentist named Painless Romaine. (Hence his tooth missing). His face (before he was christened Alfred E. Neuman) was used by several companies until he appeared regularly in Mad Magazine and they copyrighted his image. He was "born" on the cover of Mad magazine issue #29, on December, 1956.

Archie - One of the most famous and enduring cartoon characters in the world, Archie was created by Bob Montana in 1941. Archie is the typical high school student, except, of course, he's extra-special because he has red hair. The two main loves of his life, Veronica and Betty, are constantly fighting for him, enamored in his boyish good looks and charm. All of the characters in the Archie Comics, including Reggie (Archies' arch nemesis), and Archie's friend, Jughead, provide many hilarious situations for themselves and the school principal, Mr. Wetherbee. The Archie series spawned a television cartoon show and a singing group in the late 1960's.

Howdy Doody - A freckle-faced puppet that was popular on TV during the 1950's. The host of the show was Buffalo Bill, who featured other puppet characters. According to a survey, many redhead children were called "Howdy Doody" in a derisive manner throughout their childhood, causing them to dislike the wooden star.

Tommie Thompson - The most respected and levelheaded of the three female roommates in the comic strip "Apartment 3-G", Tommie Thompson is a nurse and calm personality who acts as a balance for her two other roommates, who are more flighty. The comic strip by Alex Kotzky is known for its realistic dialogue and human drama.

A classic line was delivered by a young child patient of a doctor friend of Tommie's:

"Hey, we understand how you lose track of time when you're with a beautiful redhead, but the hour was up fifteen minutes ago!"

Firestar - Female comic book Superheroine who can fly and fights by hurling fireballs. *(Marvel Comics)*

Poindexter - Redhead nerd on the "jinx" card in the game, "Barbie Goes To The Prom." *(Mattel)*

Thor, God of Thunder - Thor is an imposing flaming redhead, with bushy red eyebrows and a thick maned beard. A fearful god, he makes fire flash from his eyes and thunder roll out of the heavens when he shakes his beard.

Jabez Wilson - In the short story, "Sherlock Holmes and the Redheaded League," a redhaired man requests the help of Sherlock to solve a puzzling incident that he had experienced. Written by Sir Arthur Conan Doyle. (See "Redheaded League")

Medusa - A superwoman in the Marvel Comics, Medusa used her long red hair to fight the criminal element in the Universe.

Sheena - the She Devil - Another of the Marvel Comic Books superwomen who have redhair, Sheena dresses in an ocelot skin bikini and fights bad guys.

Princess Leigh-Cheri, Bernard Mickey Wrangle, and Nina Jablonski - These redhaired people are the main characters in Tom Robbin's eclectic "Still Life with Woodpecker." They were chased at one point by aliens from the planet, "Aragon," where redheads were thought to have escaped to Earth, because of Aragon's failing atmosphere.

As redheads settled down on other planets, including Earth and Aragon, lower human life forms tried to oppress them because of their brilliance. Fortunately, because of the greater amount of intelligent earth people, redheads have been recognized for their invaluable worth to the human race. Some excerpts:

"...Leigh-Cheri, I can't believe you were going to marry a guy with black hair."

"... persons with redhair tend to be either dangerous or funny."

"Bernard, could they really be right about redheads? Are we really moonstruck mutants whose weaknesses are betrayed by the sun?"

"The redbeards might have been connected to Mars, the red planet."

Tubby - A character created by John Stanley for the "Little Lulu" comic strip, Tubby was a roly-poly boy who was absurdedly fat. He was Lulu's best friend, constantly drawing Lulu into misadventures and causing her to find a way out of the mess.

Freckles and His Friends - A comic strip created in 1915 by Merrill Blosser, Freckles was an All-American boy who led an average but foibled life.

Flook - Originally called "Rufus," this surreal comic strip stars a redheaded boy on the search for his lost dog and wanders into other strange adventures featuring a creature who fell out of his dreams and couldn't get back. A curious strip, the creator, Wally Fawkes, sometimes inserted real-life people as characters into his plots.

Ginger Meggs - A very popular Australian comic strip, *Ginger Meggs* was the first to be syndicated overseas. Created in 1921, Ginger was a lovable redheaded schoolboy and the epitome of clear-headed thinking and homespun ideology that always seemed to work. He fought often with his enemy, an older ruffian boy by the name of Tiger Kelly. Much of his time was also spent always trying to bamboozle his other rival, Eddie Coogan, for the amours of another redhead, the pretty Minnie Peters.

Pristine De Solvo - The queen of the "Flameworld" in the comic strip, "Silver Starr in the Flameworld," Pristine was portrayed with bright redhair and blue flames glowing around her body.

Margaret - A "smarty-pants" girl with long red curls and glasses, Margaret was Dennis the Menace's foil, always asking him over for tea with her and her dolls. She snobbily delights in correcting Dennis's grammar and usually ends up either mad at him or prancing off with her nose high in the air. Dennis only likes her for the cookies she uses to bait him with in order to get him to play with her. In one cartoon, Dennis, pointing to Margaret, remarks to his little pal Joey, "Wouldn't you hate going through life being called 'carrottop'?" (Created by Hank Ketchum)

Red Fedder - A baseball player in the Mickey Finn comic strip that was popular in the 1940's. Drawn by Lank Leonard.

Red Barry - Made in likeness to gangster movies, the hero of this strip, Red Barry, was a prototype of the James Cagney tough guy character - and even was drawn to look like him. Gritty and disturbingly realistic to real-life police situations, Red Barry was a no-holds-barred comic strip that remained popular for many years after its conception in 1934 by Will Gould.

Lady Viscountess - A beautiful and charming character in "The History of Henry Esmond," by William Makepeace Thackeray, the Viscountess was always on Henry's mind from the first moment he met her. "She appeared the most charming object he had ever looked on. Her golden hair was shining in the gold of the sun; her complexion was of a dazzling bloom ..."

Red Ryder - A very popular comic strip that depicted life on a ranch in the 1890's. Once voted the most popular comic strip by the Boys Club of America, Red Ryder was a problem-solving cowboy who always did the "right thing" as he saved his adopted Navajo orphan and Sheriff Newt from threatening predicaments. Created in 1938 by Fred Harman, the name "Red Ryder" has been used in many other creations, from software to musical groups.

Rusty Riley - Rusty was a handsome lad of fourteen, who was introduced to a new world of horse racing when he ran away from an orphanage and was invited to stay on the estate of wealthy racehorse owner, Mr. Miles. The strip was considered one of the better drawn and written of its times, and many people were sad to see it end upon the death of its creator, Frank Godwin, who first drew it in 1948.

Stereotyped

In an article in the 1920 issue of "Bookman", a literary review magazine, writer Catherine Ely Beach ponders the negative characterizations of redheads in various popular novels. In her article "Are Our Novelists Fair to Redheads?" she states:

"Years of reading have convinced me that novelists have been guilty of a great injustice to a very worthy class of citizens - the redheaded."

According to Miss Beach, the novelist always makes the redhead women strikingly beautiful, but then adds the "archetype of redheaded perversity."

In men, as in works by Charles Dickens, they are portrayed as villains and usually ugly. The rumor of some is that Mr. Dickens did not favor redheads. In "David Copperfield," he wrote:

"I saw a cadaverous face appear... in the grain of it there was that tinge of red which is sometimes to be observed in the skins of redhaired people. It belonged to a redhaired person (Uriah Heep) - a youth of fifteen... his hair cropped as close as the closest stubble; who hardly had any eyebrows, and no eyelashes..."

Dickens again gives redhair to a negative character in his novel "Oliver Twist". He describes the cruel Fagin as:

"... a very old shrivelled Jew, whose villainous-looking and repulsive face was obscured by a quantity of matted red hair."

Miss Beach goes on to write about unfair representations of redheads in other writings. These include:

- Hall Caine's *The Christian*, where the character "Glory" is a robust, rollicking vampire. Having vibrant redhair and an overbearing personality, she dominates her lover with such passion that he loses his responsible nature.

- The redhaired wife and mother in the book *Helpmate*, by Mary Sinclair, tormented her child to an early death and almost succeeded killing her husband.

- Becky Sharp was a beautiful but mean-spirited girl in the novel *Vanity Fair*, by William Makepeace Thackeray. Beach states that she was "a malicious little sprite, unprincipled and incapable of affection. She has not even the merit of succeeding in her schemes, for she always overreaches herself."

- The heroine of the book *La Ferme du Choquart* by Victor Cherbuliez is a redheaded renegade who is a liar and schemer, hellbent for revenge. Her great pride edges her near insanity and she lacks "the good sense which is the most valuable ingredient in the feminine temperament."

- In *The Rise of Silas Lapham* by the gentle author Howells, the character "Irene," is a very beautiful woman with lovely redhair but is a menace to her family's well-being.

- A redhaired vixen Verena Tarrant is a prime model of selfishness as one of the characters in *The Bostonians* by Henry James.

- Edith Wharton paints a despicable portrait of a redhaired personality, Undine, in her book, *The Customs of the Country,* and cruelly refers to her redhair many times throughout the story. She intimates that Undine's beauty is "not worth the effort of any honest human being - so arid and cheap is her personality."

- In the novel *Casa Braccio* - by Marion Crawford, a redhead woman is the focus of his story, but she has no redeemable qualities and she seems intent on ruining the life of the man she loves. She involves herself in scandals which effect his work and causes great pain in her lover's life.

Catherine Ely Beach ends her article by stating: "Is it not time to halt this tradition of redheaded vampires?

Granted that red in the skin and hair indicates iron in the blood, but does not this iron, beaten to a glow by life's vicissitudes, generate energy and ambition, instead of baleful passion? Haven't you known many a redhead of excellent moral fiber and did you ever know one who was dull or worthless?"

Color Your Hair Red

The name of Polly Döge's autobiography is "Color Your Hair Red" (Hohm Press 1996). Ms. Döge isn't a redhead, but her alter-ego is. A clip: "Red-haired Stella, wearing black leather and riding behind her lover on a motorcycle along the dusty pathways of Crete, remains just out of reach, tantalizing her alter-ego with the promise of escape." The book suggests that a redhaired character is needed to embody her secret desire for a wild, passionate life.

Chapter Fourteen

RED OBSERVATIONS

"Go Big Red!"
(Battle cry of the University of Nebraska)

Many comments have been made about redheads through history, whether publicly or in a personal setting. However reflective or hysterical, these observations show the reader what an impact redhair has on others.

Judas Schmoodas

"Redheads should wear wigs to hide the color of their hair, of which everybody stands in horror because Judas, it is said, was redhaired."
(From the 17th Century book *Histoire des Perruques* [a history of wigs])

Red Sacrifice

"The red hair of these unfortunates was probably significant. For in Egypt, the oxen which were sacrificed also had to be red, a single black or white hair on the beast would have disqualified it for the sacrifice. If, as I conjecture, these human sacrifices were intended to promote the growth of crops, and the winnowing of ashes seems to support this view, redhaired victims were perhaps selected as best fitted

to personate the spirit of the ruddy grain. For, when a god is represented by a living person, it is natural that the human representative should be chosen on the grounds of his supposed resemblance to the divine original."
(Sir James Frazer, from *The Golden Bough*)

Red Scent

Augustin Galopin of France wrote in his book, "Le Parrum de la Femme," published in 1886, that redheads have much stronger natural body scents than brunettes and blondes. They smell like *"the perfumes of violets or amber,"* according to his research.

Dizzy Red

"Anyhow, it is a definite color: I am glad I have redhair. There it is in the mirror, it makes itself seen, it shines. I am still lucky: If my forehead was surmounted by one of those neutral heads of hair which are neither chestnut nor blond, my face would be lost in vagueness, it would make me dizzy."
(Jean-Paul Sartre, *Nausea*)

Red Widow Spider

> *"Out of the ash*
> *I rise with my redhair*
> *and I eat men like air."*
>
> (Sylvia Plath from *Lady Lazarus*)

Make The Kids Happy!

"Children often hate their red hair because they tend to place a high premium on conformity, and redheads make up just 5% of America's population."
(Al Sacharov, author of *The Redhead Book*)

Make the Red Choice

"REDHAIRED WOMEN - Fair haired ladies claim to make the most affectionate wives; but he who marries a redhaired woman would do well not to be remiss in his attentions, for they woo warmly, and expect to be warmly wooed. A French woman with redhair is a rare occurrence, but wherever there is one, love has a decided votary."*
(*votary, n. one who is devoted or engaged by a promise)
(*Mysteries and Revelations in Love, Courtship, and Marriage*, by Eugene Becklard, M.D. [1844])

Shades of Sherlock!

"Every shade of colour they were – straw, lemon, orange, brick, Irishsetter, clay; but as Spaulding said there were not many who had the real vivid flame-coloured tint."
(*The Redheaded League - Sherlock Holmes*, by A.C. Doyle)

"Red is the most positive of colors."
(Man, Myth and Magic)

Red Light

In 1986 on a segment of the "Phil Donahue Show," a high-class madam was featured talking about her girls. She stated that "my redhaired girls are the hardest to place (least desired or asked for.)"

Always Innocent

"You will please describe the boy to me. Was he redheaded?" (asked Flynn).

The pawnbroker blinked.

"Of course he wasn't redheaded," said Flynn. "That would make it too easy for me. Redheads learn early enough in life to never commit crimes in front of witnesses."

(Police Inspector Francis Flynn to a pawnbroker in the novel, *Flynn,* by Greg McDonald)

Wheel Red

"You could see he thought redheads were hell on wheels."

(Franklin Charles, *The Vice Czar Murders*)

Red Sense

"The lure of redhair is far more primitive than the prosy mathematics of supply and demand. Red is the color of heat, of wine, of blood. . . It is both a

welcome and a warning, and even the most civilized man feels a curiously atavistic quickening of the sense at the sight of a redhaired woman . . . there's a lot to be learned by observing the avant-red-garde."
(*Vogue* - 1969)

Red Religion

The reddish, waving, abundant hair resembles the sun gods, nearly all of them being represented with an abundance of long, waving, red or yellow hair, denoting the rays of the sun.
(*Aryan Sun Myths – The Origin of Religions*)

"When redhaired people are above a certain social grade, their hair is auburn."
(Observation by Mark Twain)

Howdy Rudely

(From the comic strip "CATHY," by Cathy Guisewite)
FRIEND: (reading from a singles ad) "So you need physical descriptions before you'll meet someone, Cathy? Fine... (Here's one)"Receding hairline, squinty eyes, smirks a lot"....
CATHY: Bleah. Forget him.
FRIEND: That was Bruce Willis.
CATHY: Bruce? Wait... Bruce?
FRIEND: How about "Scrawny, big mouth, likes to rip his clothes off..."
CATHY: Bleah. Forget him.
FRIEND: That was Mick Jagger. How about "Reddish hair. Cute face, always smiling"...
CATHY: Yes! I'll take him! Yes!
FRIEND: Howdy Doody.

Chapter Fifteen

HAPPY REDHEADS

"Our family is very proud of being redheaded and feel that it's only passed down to the special children in it."
Laura B., Berkeley, Ca.

"To me, being a redhead is a special gift from God - your own little spotlight, a touch, a beautiful individuality. I enjoy my special gift to the fullest!"
Tammy Jean B., Dallas, Texas

"Do you know what they say about redheads? Redheads do what blondes think about!"'
Karen Bums, Ca.

"Being a tall (6'5") redhead has always given me great satisfaction! I enjoy my individuality and uniqueness and my ability to stick out in a crowd."
Barry M., Los Angeles, Ca.

"When the Main Man (God) made the (perfect human), He wanted to put something on them so they would stand out in a crowd, so he gave them redhair. That's why there are so few of us, we don't want the others (non-redheads) to feel inferior. Just enough of us for them to stand up and take notice. Redheads, hold your head high for the eyes of the rest of the world are upon us."
Grant B. C., Greeley, Co.

"Thank God for the pretty redhead, Even if much later we learn, Just what a fiery temper they have, But we love our Glinda Laverne."
Mary Sanchez, Santa Ana, Ca.

"They say that blonds have more fun,
And that may well be true,
But when the calculating is done
Redheads sure come through"
By Maree Blizard, Sheffield, Texas

"Blondes and brunettes are a dime a dozen
but a redhead is worth a fortune!"
and,
"Men prefer blondes, They marry brunettes,
and the 'other woman' is usually a redhead."
Anonymous

"Blondes may have more fun, but redheads ARE!"
Cheryl G., Ohio

"Redheads can be as refreshing as strawberries and cream on a hot summer day... we must be gentle with those non-natural redheads who try so desperately to imitate us. There will still be enough to enable people to distinguish us from non-natural redheads: our vivacious personalities."
Toddrico B., Hartford, Ct.

"The beauty of a redhead not only lies in the amazing color, but often goes much deeper. All the redheads I've known are fun-loving, talented, and have great senses of humor. A lot of this comes from the pains of growing up and trying to overcome whatever problems arise from the prejudices."
Tricia F., Redding, California

"I met my husband on a blind date, and when he found out that I had red hair, he didn't want to meet me. He went on the date anyways, and it turned out to be his red-letter day!"
Kelly M., California

My brother has four children who all have very red hair. When he comes back from a business trip at the airport and four little redheads scream "Daddy!" and start running toward him, the people in the area just grin from ear to ear. When we go to a restaurant, his wife and I let them all go ahead of us and then we just stand back and watch the reactions of the other patrons!"
M. J. C., Lincoln, Nebraska

"My Grandma Dittmer, a beautician, always said if you have beautiful hair, always show it off to its best advantage so everyone will notice it. '"
Virgene T., Ohio

"When I was a little girl, I used to cry when people called me names because I had redhair. Now I am a 75-year young lady and I am proud of my red hair. I hold my head high now, but do get mad when some people think I color my hair (I do not)."
Ruth E. B., Maine

"Red hair is original"
Kristine L., Minnesota

"I'm a true redhead, and I must say I am proud of it. This was not always true. I used to feel sorry for anyone who was born with redhair. But now I feel lucky because I was born with a unique hair color."
Terry D., Oklahoma

"Due to the low population percentage of redheads, I feel that people have a generally negative attitude towards red hair and I would love to see that attitude changed so people will realize that redheads are no different than blondes or brunettes. I think this attitude is gradually changing as redheads are becoming more and more noticed (in fashion) ... it is an easy (positive) way to be different in this world where there is a lot of emphasis on individuality."
Kim J., New York

"I am twelve years old, a Taurus, and I am told that I am very stubborn and headstrong. Must be because of my redhot temper. My temper is redder and hotter than my hair and it is set off by a hair trigger. My sister is an expert at pulling the trigger. The reason I have redhair is because I am a descendant of Eric the Red."
Corrine S., Alberta, Canada

"Move over blondes,
Step back brunettes,
Here come the redheads!'
Cookie E., Ca.

"Like other redheads, I too, have been unmercifully beaten with names, though in truth I feel a positive character has emerged as a result and I've grown to appreciate and love the individuality it gives me."
Janet K, Massachusetts

"I envision scholarships for us, special parking privileges, a beauty contest, a college, special hair salons, a redheaded nation free from oppression. Lead our people to the promised land! Hallelujah!"
Chris L, Calif. on learning of Redheads International, a club for redheads.

From an eight year-old redhaired girl, Karissa E. of California, whose father and sister are also redhaired: *"My mom is having a baby. We hope it is a redhead!"* (She now has a redheaded brother)

"There are people who prefer red to another color. Although I am a brunette, never does a redhead go by without turning my head. (Redheads) should be pleased to know that there are people like me around applauding them."
Karen I., California

"People always expect more from a girl with naturally curly red hair... and they get it!"
Bonnie P., Michigan

"I am a redhead and so is my daughter. I go to school to learn to be a hairdresser, and when fellow students put color on their hair and they goof up and it comes out red, they PANIC! I really have to laugh to myself!"
(an Olympia, Washington redhead)

"There is not one day that goes by that I am not glad that I have red hair!"
Jean W., Pennsylvania

Chapter Sixteen

REDHEADS IN THE NEWS

Redheaded Delivery Man

October 7, 1986 - A cargo plane was shot down by Nicaraguan troops who suspected that it was dropping off supplies for the Contras. One man parachutes out of the plane and survives, but is picked up by the troops who hold him captive. In the news article as reported by the Los Angeles Times, the man, Eugene Hasenfus, is an ex-marine with no proven CIA ties. The article features an interesting quote from his aunt. "He is a very handsome gentleman," she said. "He has red hair and the greatest smile you would ever want to see. Blue eyes, some freckles, a real neat looking guy."

At his trial, he was convicted of running guns and supplies and given a thirty-year sentence, but was pardoned by the Sandinista leader, President Ortega, and he returned to the United States within a few days.

Not So Happiest Place on Earth

"REDHEADS - HAVE - LESS - FUN - LAND" - Thus ran a heading in the Los Angeles Times (Calendar Section - 7/14/85). In May, 1984, Victoria Penley claims in a pending lawsuit she was refused permission to enter the Disneyland park because the style and color of her redhair was deemed "inappropriate." Penley, 39, said the color and style of her hair were the same as when she was the principal of a school for handicapped children.

"I'm a redhead," she stated. "I have had this color hair since I was 10... It's the color of Lucille Ball's, only it's not so carroty." [Another incident was reported that a girl with a punkish red hairdo was refused admittance for the same reason a few months earlier.]

Red Wave

"Dear Abby:

For the last six months I have worked in a movie theatre in San Francisco, and I feel that I do a very good job. Last week I changed my hair color from brown to red. It looks very natural - not 'punk' or 'new wave.' Just red. Anyways, here's the problem: My manager thinks it is awful and I should change it back immediately. I think he is overstepping his bounds as manager to even suggest such a thing. Do you think I should bow to his wishes, or do what I want with my hair. I'm a male, if that makes a difference."

Signed, *Red and Fuming*

Dear *Red*:

Male or female, it's your right to change the color of your hair. And if, as you say, it looks "natural" and not "punk or new wave", your manager is indeed overstepping his bounds in suggesting that you change it back immediately.
(From the LA TIMES, 6/23/83)

What About the Stork?

"Dear Abby:
I am a natural blonde and my husband's hair is black. We have a 3-year-old who's hair is flaming red. We've heard all the snide remarks about mailmen, traveling salesmen, etc., but what would our daughter say when people ask her where she got her redhair?"

Signed, *Stymied in Sacramento*

Dear *STYMIED*:
A Tulsa reader gave me the ideal retort: "When our son was about 4 years-old, and people would ask him where he got his redhair, we taught him to say, 'It came with my head.'"
(From the LA TIMES 6/2/86)

Redfaced for a Redhead

Helen Raptis, an attractive redhead, has an interesting job; she works the microphones for the House of Representatives in Montana. She controls the volume as each representative begin to speak. While attempting to talk, Rep. Fred Thomas, (R-Stephensville), tapped the microphone and asked,
"Am I on? Am I turned on?" Seeing the attractive Ms. Raptis start to adjust the volume for him, Rep. Thomas muttered, "I'd like to turn you on!"
His little comment was blasted over the house speakers as Raptis had turned the volume up too far. Rep. Thomas stood there speechless, his face blazing with embarrassment.

Several days later, when Rep. Thomas rose to debate on another issue, the House Chairman asked Raptis, "Is Rep. Thomas turned on?"

"I hope so," Ms. Raptis replied, causing the Montana legislature to break out in uproarious laughter. *(Source - The Associated Press)*

Sicko

In 1985, a man was arrested for suspicion of murder in the deaths of eleven redhaired women. Charles Miller, 28, was convicted of at least one murder and sentenced to life in prison. His victims, all redhaired, were usually picked up hitchhiking and were murdered along the highways in several different states, stretching from Texas to Pennsylvania. *(Source - Associated Press)*

Playboy Magazine

In 1983, Playboy Magazine did a pictorial on redheads. Several positive letters to the editor commenting on the pictorial were printed in the following issue. However, one letter (below) was filled with animosity:

"I am surprised that you chose to feature redheads in your October issue. Women with redhair are the least popular with men. They have a reputation for being vile, stubborn and negative. Besides, who wants a woman who is covered with freckles or unable to tan? You mention that Lucille Ball is a redhead. I suppose she typifies the image that redheads emulate to make

up for their weaknesses. However, you fail to mention two other redheads - Judas Iscariot and Lenin."
L.J. Rohr, Cuyahoga Falls, Ohio.

To which Playboy's editor replied: "
What's the matter, LJ.? Did you get kicked out of Ireland?"

Dear Abby Again

In response to a survey among 1,000 men on whether 'gentlemen preferred blondes' (redheads came in last, blondes were first), Dear Abby took her own informal poll while on a plane flight to Los Angeles. One man wrote, "You asked the wrong man. My wife is sitting right next to me and, as you can see, she is a natural redhead. She also has a fiery temper to match, so naturally this gentleman definitely wouldn't look twice at a blonde."
(Dear Abby- LA Times 10/30/86)

Ron, Darling

Ron Darling, the lead pitcher for the New York Mets during their World Series winning season of 1986, married Toni O'Reilly, a beautiful redhaired Wilhelmina model. Interviewed in a "People" magazine article, he stated, *"If anyone ever told me I would marry a redhead, I would have said he was crazy. Redheads have freckles."*

Eileen Ford No Award

Eileen Ford, co-founder of the Ford Modeling Agency in New York City, slighted redheads in a "People" magazine article (5/16/83) by stating that *"too bad redhair doesn't sell... and it's not good to have freckles."* Asked about her statements in a following newspaper interview, she stated, *"I've been in this business for (many) years, and redheads are a dead market, and always will be."*

The club Redheads International vowed to prove her wrong, and after three years of promoting redhead events and redheads, Ms. Ford's concessions were printed worldwide in a 1986 UPI article by Melissa Sones. *"Redhair is slowly coming into style. More and more redheads are being booked... It's been a hard sell for me,"* Ford admitted.

McDonalds

After Evelyn Schultz of the Wormser, Heldfond & Joseph Theatrical Agency was reported saying in a 1983 Los Angeles Times article that *"every time we do a McDonald's commercial, we're told 'no redheads' and no freckles. Maybe that's because Ronald McDonald has redhair."* After the article was printed, McDonald's suddenly began featuring an abundance of redheads in their commercials.

The Un-Red Writer

"Backstage, many of the women cast suspicious green eyes at some of their peers' heads. There were tall reds, tiny reds, chubby red, scrawny reds, classy reds, cheapo reds, even a deaf red."

(An excerpt from an article by Gerald Nachman, a writer for the San Francisco Chronicle, in an August 7, 1986 story on the Redheads International Beauty Pageant. The "deaf red" he referred to won 2nd runner-up, one of the first handicapped women to win a beauty pageant in America.

Too Red

"Though none of us has any control over the attributes we are born with, a child is often ridiculed because of his physical appearance. His peers find him too short or too tall or say that his ears stick out, his hair is too red, his nose is too big." (From an article "Mommy, It's Not Fair!" in the 1985 February edition of the *Ladies Home Journal*)

Redheads in the Library

Helena Negrette held a show at the Jones Library in Amherst, Massachusetts, that featured her photographs of local redheads and other information on redheads. Her presentation of redhaired glory was called: "Redheads: A Secret Nation." The show ran from March 1 - 31, 1984.
(Source - Daily Hampshire Gazette, 2/28/84)

Redheads on the Mural

Famous photographer, Joel Meyerowitz was commissioned by the H.J. Heinz Company in 1985 to produce a work of art for their collection. His choice of work turned out to be a 8-foot photographic mural of a beach landscape covered with only redheaded people of all ages. The models were members of Redheads International. The mural was displayed in the New York Museum of Modern Art and later in a book called "Redheads," featuring a collection of photos by Meyerowitz. He used the same photos for a pictorial book called "Redheads," published in 1986.

New York is a Redhead

The author of an article "The Redhaired City," which appeared in the April 27, 1927, issue of the "Atlantic Monthly," would lead the reader to believe that she is in great admiration of redheads. She writes as follows:

"A beautiful redhaired woman stands out even among other beautiful women, as she possesses something they do not, which would exercise an instant and irresistible fascination...

"Is not redhair, in a beautiful woman, the final touch of wonder? Does it not lift the possessor up and out above her rivals, render her visibly sister and daughter of the sun?

"Does it not make even the moderately pretty in form and features pass as lovely, and the generously gifted add wonder and excitement? Fashion may veer and change, but redhair is independent of it...

"If a man says he dislikes it, he is paying inverted tribute to something primitive in himself which at once thrills him and makes him afraid...

"... in some way, the redhead woman is different, and the difference goes deeper than the pigmentation of her hair. That it is not only the color can easily be proved. No one has ever felt either mystery or attraction in red hair in men.

Redheaded boys are described as carroty; redheaded

men cut their hair exceptionally short, as if in the hope of concealing it.

"... in a man it has no distinct significance - none of the significance it has in a woman ...

"But I believe that if the redhaired women one knows are submitted to an impartial comparative scrutiny, it will be found there is something difficult to define, impossible not to feel, which all of them lack."

"... Until one gets near, probes deep, cares much, one may not discover it; but as one does one will. There is something inaccessible, something that does not respond."

"There is a word for this thing the redhaired woman has not got... a soul. The redhaired woman has no soul... there is no other form of words which will cover their peculiarities except that which declares that they have no souls."

"As happens when one meets a lovely redhaired woman, fear and admiration mingle in the mind: more than a touch of envy, and, behind that, a hesitating doubt. New York has so much that one boggles at saying that anything is missing; and yet this sense of something missing will persist.

"So New York seems to me to have what the redhaired woman has and to miss what she misses... Is there, here, a blind spot, like the blind spot in the redhaired woman who hurts the man who loves her?

"... (So) They wait for New York. Her red hair will turn gray. In that process she may lose something. But out of it her soul will come to birth."

"Redhair isolates you." Actress Myrna Loy

Chapter Seventeen

QUOTATIONS FROM THE PAST

Some of the following quotations were excerpted from the *Oxford Dictionary of English (Large Volume)*. It is a huge volume of writing, and a recommended source for anyone interested in early European interpretations or language.

"... your color... as red as any rose."
Shakespeare - Henry IV, [1589]

"His berd (beard) as any sowe or fox, was reed"
Thomas Chaucer- 1386

"Thou shaft know a lewde fellow
by his beard eyther red or yealow."
Withals - 1584

"His hair is of the dissembling color,
something browner than Judas'."
Shakespeare - 1599

"... the Red is wise, the Brown trusty, the Pale envious, and the Black lusty." (speaking of beards) From *Blazon of Jealousie,* by R. Tofte - 1615

"He is false by nature that has a black head and a red beard."
Fuller - 1732

"Greete a redde man and bearded women three myles Off."
Sanford - 1573

"A red cow gives good milk."
Compleat Angler - 1917

"Aenobarbus ... a roman so callyd because he had a berde as red as brasse."
Elyot Addit - 1538

"... he had a jolly long redpeake (beard) he cherisht continually without cutting."
Nashe - 1593

"Thou art a proper man if thy beard is redder."
From *Love's Cure*, by Fletcher - 1625

"The hair... from being slightly tinged with yellow, assumes... that particular which is, more commonly than correctly, termed red."
Pinckard - 1797

"Ho - so hath furye mest he is smal and red."
Ibid. - 319/686 A.D.

"Tho that bene rede men bene trechurus and likenyd to foxis."
Ibid- 1422

"It is observed that the redhaired of both sexes are more libidinous and mischievous than the rest."
From *Gulliver's Travels*, by Jonathan Swift

"... the redhaired Charioteer of the day."
T. Brown, (referring to the sun) 1704

"You see Man divided into groups of blackheads (the race of Ham) and redheads (the race of Adam)."
Kohler- 1893

"No such Orators againe, as redheaded Angelles."
Harvey- 1580

"He has made me smell for all the world like a flax, or a redheaded woman's chamber."
From the *Fatal Dowry*, by Massinger & Field - 1632

"A redheaded man never squeals."
From the play called the "Outing" - 1889

"Any color so long as it's red."
From Eugene Field's *Red* - 1885

"The flaming red denotes a callous mind too harsh for love or sentiment refined."
Charles Stearns - *The Ladies Philosophy of Love* - 1797

"Red hair does not carry its owner to Heaven, but as a help through life few things are better."
Journey of the Flame

Chapter Eighteen

REDHEAD RESPECT

The remarks in this section are made by either journalists in their articles or others whose statements are not really considered to be true revelations or facts about redheads, just their heartfelt declarations about them. These statements were made for the purpose of augmentation to the positive redhead theme.

An unnamed London scientist once remarked, *"Redhaired people are highly intelligent. They have many admirers, and they marry young."*
(Article by Carl Schurz Lowden)

"A redheaded woman can make a choo-choo jump its tracks"
(George Gershwin, popular songwriter)

"I think all of them (redhaired men) have, or have had a possession, a bravura and a determination to impose. Violets they are not."
(quote by the author Edna O'Brien from an article called "Ginger" - printed in the "Tattler" -1985)

"Redheads are big on horses"
(Ibid.)

"...blond hair as an eye-catcher cannot often hold a candle to red hair's flame. Nonetheless, redheads persist as too small a minority to have asserted a strong presence over the years. What redhead tradition exists, in fact, is mostly negative, imposed entirely by brownheads. Which is unfortunate and decidedly unfair."
(Jeremy Schlosberg, columnist for "Upstate Magazine" in a 1983 issue)

"Blondes and brunettes are establishment. Redheads are fashion."
(Frances Grill, NY's Click Modeling Agency - 1986)

"...But red! Oh, red is perfect! I'd be just eternally overjoyed if my hair was red, or at least auburn. But since I'll never have naturally redhair, I guess I'll have to settle for a redheaded husband. Therefore, I'm always on the lookout for nice, tall, thin guys with redhair. I get teased for this ambition by my friends a lot.
(from a letter to Redheads International by brown-haired 15-year-old Julie A., of Shreveport, La.)

"There she was, red hair and the biggest blue eyes I've ever seen!"
(Alan Ladd describing Arlene Dahl in the movie "Desert Legion")

"Har, you lousy sorrel-top!"
(*My Southern Friends*, J.R. Gilmore - 1863)

Chapter Nineteen

RUMORED REDHEADS

These people are thought to have been redheads, but there is no substantiation in which to say with some certainty. In earlier days of history, anyone with fair skin and lighter hair, usually more reddish or blonder than dark brown was sometimes referred to as being ruddish, meaning "red-colored."

Jezebel - the Pagan Queen of Israel who lost the war against the prophet Elijah in the Old Testament.

Mary Magdalene - friend of Jesus Christ

Jesus Christ - Son of God. It is said that he had deep burgundy hair the color of wine.

Nero - Crazy and sadistic ruler of Rome during its last days.

Wild Bill Hickock - Gunfighter, buffalo hunter, and Indian scout.

Dwight Eisenhower - Five Star General and President of the United States, who used to be called "Red Ike" by his classmates in high school.

Thomas Hardy - English author and poet, who during his time was well-known, albeit controversial, for his sympathetic leanings towards matters considered immoral for his day.

REDHEADS BY CHOICE

Angela Lansbury - A respected actress for over three decades, Angela Lansbury most always was cast as someone's mother or the friend of the female star character. She won two Tony awards in her well-rounded career on stage and in films, and became the star of her own television series, "Murder, She Wrote", which has been a popular series running for over ten years.

Other redheads by choice:

Julia Prowse
Barbara Streisand
Victoria Principal
Stephanie Edwards

(Author's note: *It is quiet impossible to follow the hair coloring habits of the famous, but the above women are commonly known to have redhair at some point in their careers. The author does not have control over future hues they choose to dabble in.*)

FINAL WORD UNTIL TOMORROW

I want to see everyone happy and feeling great about themselves, which is the beginning of self-respect and the respect of others. I have tried to gather enough information to satisfy all of you redheads and redhead admirers. If I have failed in my attempt, please write to me and let me know what I have omitted, forgotten about, listed incorrectly or was just plain ignorant in explaining here. I welcome your comments, adulation, or ripostes. Please let me know of any new redhead information you come across. Send the information in and if I use it, I will send you a free copy of the next edition of --

THE REDHEAD ENCYCLOPEDIA !

Stephen Douglas

Redheads International
537 Newport Center Drive #119
Newport Beach, CA 92660

BIBLIOGRAPHY

Tattler/Edna O 'Brien;
The Little, Brown Book of Anecdotes
The Book of People, Christopher P. Andersen / Perigee Books 1981
Encyclopedia Americana
Chambers Biographical Dictionary
The Great Quotations, compiled by George Seldes
Notable American Women - The Modern Period
Legends of the World, by Richard Cavendish
New Century Cyclopedia of Names
Marquis's Who's Who in America; LA Times 2/14/85;
The Boston Globe 1982
Kingdoms of Europe, by Gene Gurney
Who's Who in Hollywood, by David Ragan
(Maureen O'Hara) Baltimore News-Post 2/23/55)
(Janet Gaynor) Dallas Times Herald, 9/15/84)
Joe Franklin's Encyclopedia of Comedians
(Venus Ramey) Sue Gilmore/Sacramento Union 7/15/84
Man, Myth and Magic, by Marshall Carendish
Dictionary of Classical Mythology, by Robert E. Bell
Encyclopedia of Fairies, by Katharine Briggs
"Boke of Curtasye," 15th Century
Brewer's Dictionary of Phrase and Fable, by Ivan Evans
Superstition and the Superstitious, by Eric Maple
Standard Dictionary of Folklore, Mythology and Legend
The Trivia Encyclopedia, by Fred Worth
Halliwell's Film Guide
Popular Song Index, by Patricia Havlice
The Oxford Dictionary of English Etymology
Scots Dictionary, by Alexander Warrack
Psychology Today 2/83, by Carol Krucoff
The Art of the Comic Strip, by Shirley Glubok
The World Encyclopedia of Comics, by Maurice Horn
A Smithsonian Book of Comic Book Comics
Classic Comics and their Creators, by Martin Sheridan
The MacMillan Book of Proverbs, Maxims, and Famous Phrases, by
    Stevenson
The Redhead Book, by Al Sacharov
The Skin, A Clinopathologic Treatise, by Allan Arthur
Red Hair in African Negroes: A Preliminary Study (*Annals of Eugenics*),
    1953, by NA Barnicot
The Pigment Trichosiderin, from Human Red Hair, (*Nature*)
The Relation of the Pigment Trichosiderin to Hair Colour, (*Annals of Human
    Genetics*)
The Structure and Formation of Pigment Granules in Human Hair
    (*Experimental Cell Research*), by M. Birbeck
The First Human Hair Symposium, Dr. Algie C. Brown
Isolation of an Iron Pigment from Human Red Hair, (*Journal of Investigative
    Dermatology*)

Red Hair Colour as a Genetical Character, (*Annals of Eugenics*) 1952, by T. E. Reed

Inheritance of Red Hair fo Six Generations (*The Journal of Heredity*) - 1964, by Ralph Singleton, Brenda Ellis

Strange Stories, Amazing Facts (*Readers Digest*) - 1976

Hyperactive Behaviour in Redheaded Children, (*Eugenics Society Bulletin*) - 1980, Michael Bar, Yitshak Wintner, Shamai Davidson

The People's Almanac Presents the Book of Lists, by David Wallechinsky, Irving Wallace and Amy Wallace

William Lyon Mackenzie, Rebel against Authority (1971) Flint, David

The Firebrand: William Lyon Mackenzie and the Rebellion in Upper Canada (1956).Kilbourn, William

The Mystery of Easter Island, by Katherine Routeledge

Myth And Symbol in Ancient Egypt, by Clark Rundle

Improving Your Child's Behavior Chemistry, by Dr. Lendon Smith

Irish Druids and Old Irish Religions, by James Bonwick

Bullfinches Mythology, by Thomas Bullfinch

The Viking Explorers, by Frederick Pohl

Christopher Columbus, by Daniel Sargent

Thomas Jefferson, the Complete Man, by James Eichner

Portrait of Emily Dickinson, by David Higgins

Margaret Sanger, Pioneer of Birth Control, by Lader, Lawrence, Meltzer, Milton

Van Gogh: A Study of His Life and Work, by Frank Elgar

Elizabeth I, by Joseph Levine

Winston Churchill, by Victor Albjerg

Sun Lore of All Ages, by William Olcott

Story of Jesus, Based on the Edgar Cayce Readings, by Clifford Owens

INDEX

MORE REDHEAD NEWS !

If you like redheads or being redheaded, don't miss out on the fabulous _Redhott Redheads Video_, a two-hour compilation of redhead beauty pageants and events. It's a world of redheads!

Want bumperstickers, buttons and other redhead promotional items? Want to join other redheads in a flame-haired celebration? Join our worldwide club, _Redheads International_, and receive our quarterly newsletter, _The Redheader!_ You'll get updates and new facts on the fabulous culture of redheads!

For more information on how to get all this cool redheaded stuff, write to:

Redheads International™
537 Newport Center Drive
Newport Beach, CA 92660